The Politics of East European Area Studies

Following the end of the Cold War and European Union enlargement, in what sense does Eastern Europe continue to exist as a meaningful geo-political concept? In addressing this question, contributors to this volume – Robert Bideleux, Alex Cistelecan, Katalin Miklóssy and Dieter Segert – tease out the implications for an "Area Studies" approach to the region. They examine its contradictory situation within discourses of "orientalization": on one hand, posited as the "underdeveloped" pendant to its western neighbours; on the other, largely Christian by religion and an integral part of a continent that dominated the world. They uncover the roots of area studies in the "colonial paradigm" by which great powers promote the creation of predictive, "problem-solving" knowledge that is immediately apprehendable for decision-makers, helping them to take advantage of a region's resources and strategic position, but which tends to homogenize the region's geography and history. For critical inquiry, they argue, the challenge is to delineate transparently the reasons underlying Eastern Europe's construction as an area of study, to identify the epistemological interests of motivated organizations such as funding agencies and political bodies, and to counter the ongoing orientalism of Western perspectives toward the East.

This book was originally published as a special issue of the *Journal of Contemporary Central and Eastern Europe*.

Gareth Dale teaches Politics at Brunel University. He has published on Karl Polanyi, Eastern Europe and the GDR, green growth and international migration. Recent publications include *First the Transition, then the Crash: Eastern Europe in the 2000s* (2011) and *Karl Polanyi: The Limits of the Market* (2010).

Katalin Miklóssy teaches Eastern European Area Studies at the University of Helsinki, with a particular focus on issues related to democratisation. She has published on competition, modernization and Cold War interactions regarding East Central European countries.

Dieter Segert teaches Eastern European Area Studies at Vienna University. He has published chapters and articles in numerous books and journals on state socialism and its legacy, democracy and party politics.

The Politics of East European Area Studies

Edited by
Gareth Dale, Katalin Miklóssy and
Dieter Segert

LONDON AND NEW YORK

First published 2016
by Routledge
2 Park Square, Milton Park, Abingdon, Oxon, OX14 4RN, UK

and by Routledge
711 Third Avenue, New York, NY 10017, USA

Routledge is an imprint of the Taylor & Francis Group, an informa business

© 2016 Taylor & Francis

All rights reserved. No part of this book may be reprinted or reproduced or utilised in any form or by any electronic, mechanical, or other means, now known or hereafter invented, including photocopying and recording, or in any information storage or retrieval system, without permission in writing from the publishers.

Trademark notice: Product or corporate names may be trademarks or registered trademarks, and are used only for identification and explanation without intent to infringe.

British Library Cataloguing in Publication Data
A catalogue record for this book is available from the British Library

ISBN 13: 978-1-138-65330-6

Typeset in TrebuchetMS
by RefineCatch Limited, Bungay, Suffolk

Publisher's Note
The publisher accepts responsibility for any inconsistencies that may have arisen during the conversion of this book from journal articles to book chapters, namely the possible inclusion of journal terminology.

Disclaimer
Every effort has been made to contact copyright holders for their permission to reprint material in this book. The publishers would be grateful to hear from any copyright holder who is not here acknowledged and will undertake to rectify any errors or omissions in future editions of this book.

Contents

Citation Information	vii
Notes on Contributors	ix

1. Introduction   . 1
   Gareth Dale, Katalin Miklóssy and Dieter Segert

2. The "Orientalization" and "de-Orientalization" of East Central
   Europe and the Balkan Peninsula   7
   Robert Bideleux

3. From Region to Culture, from Culture to Class   43
   Alex Cistelecan

4. Russian and East European Studies with a Finnish Flavour   59
   Katalin Miklóssy

5. Is There Really Something Like "Eastern Europe"? And If So,
   Why Do We Need Area Studies of It?   79
   Dieter Segert

    Index   95

Citation Information

The following chapters were originally published in the *Journal of Contemporary Central and Eastern Europe*, volume 23, issue 1 (April 2015). When citing this material, please use the original page numbering for each article, as follows:

Chapter 2
The "Orientalization" and "de-Orientalization" of East Central Europe and the Balkan Peninsula
Robert Bideleux
Journal of Contemporary Central and Eastern Europe, volume 23, issue 1 (April 2015) pp. 9–44

Chapter 3
From Region to Culture, from Culture to Class
Alex Cistelecan
Journal of Contemporary Central and Eastern Europe, volume 23, issue 1 (April 2015) pp. 45–60

Chapter 4
Russian and East European Studies with a Finnish Flavour
Katalin Miklóssy
Journal of Contemporary Central and Eastern Europe, volume 23, issue 1 (April 2015) pp. 61–80

Chapter 5
Is There Really Something Like "Eastern Europe"? And If So, Why Do We Need Area Studies of It?
Dieter Segert
Journal of Contemporary Central and Eastern Europe, volume 23, issue 1 (April 2015) pp. 81–96

For any permission-related enquiries please visit:
http://www.tandfonline.com/page/help/permissions

Notes on Contributors

Robert Bideleux is a reader (associate professor) in Politics and International Relations at Swansea University, UK. His main publications are *Communism and Development* (Routledge, 2014), (with Ian Jeffries) *A History of Eastern Europe* (Routledge, 2007) and *The Balkans: a Post-Communist History* (Routledge, 2007). He runs a PPE degree programme and teaches and researches on political economy, history of economic thought, European integration, governance, Central and East Europe, Brazil, post-colonialism and genocide.

Alex Cistelecan is a lecturer at Petru Maior University, Romania, and editor at criticatac.ro.

Gareth Dale teaches Politics at Brunel University. He has published on Karl Polanyi, Eastern Europe and the GDR, green growth and international migration. Recent publications include *First the Transition, then the Crash: Eastern Europe in the 2000s* (2011) and *Karl Polanyi: The Limits of the Market* (2010).

Katalin Miklóssy teaches Eastern European Area Studies at the University of Helsinki, with a particular focus on issues related to democratization. She has published on competition, modernization and Cold War interactions regarding East Central European countries.

Dieter Segert teaches Eastern European Area Studies at Vienna University. He has published chapters and articles in numerous books and journals on state socialism and its legacy, democracy and party politics.

Introduction

Gareth Dale, Katalin Miklóssy and Dieter Segert

Area Studies are on the verge of change. Inherited concepts that once served to aggregate countries within regions are being re-examined, as is the art of studying them. This volume explores the construction and present existence of Eastern Europe: where it is situated, what are the fundaments of its identity and how it has been apprehended as a subject of "area studies" analysis. Four authors – Robert Bideleux, Alex Cistelecan, Katalin Miklóssy and Dieter Segert – seek to make sense of the political and cultural identity of Eastern Europe in the current conjuncture. Following the end of the Cold War and the ongoing process of EU enlargement, they ask in what sense does Eastern Europe continue to exist as a meaningful geopolitical concept? With its western segments subsumed within the European Union, have all salient commonalities with the "rest" disappeared – except insofar as they too aspire to membership of the club? In addressing these questions, they tease out the implications for an Area Studies approach to the region, asking how the nature and evolution of Area Studies has affected the scholarly lens. In this introduction, we sketch the terrain of this debate, situating the major topics to be explored in the chapters that follow.

To begin with the most distant background, let us briefly consider Europe and the evolution of its eastern segment. A geopolitical oddity, this corner of Eurasia came superciliously to self-identify as a continent, within a process charged by the interaction of empire and religion. Under Rome, imperial geography had organized itself around the Mediterranean, but as Roman power frayed, the coordinates shifted: its anointed religion was maintained in the northern and western provinces, some Greek and Roman traditions were preserved by the Byzantine Empire, and Islam spread throughout the South and the East. Within this broad transformation, Europe as a cultural idea arose, inspired, along one vector, by the unity of previously warring Christian factions in common crusades against Islam; along another, by Europe's post-Columbian colonization of the rest of the world – to which moment, as Bideleux points out, Europe owes its racialization. In the same period – the first half of the last millennium – another imperial process was furrowing the region: the Mongol incursions and conquests. As Perry Anderson has argued (218), their pattern and frequency "made them one of the basic coordinates" of the formation of *Eastern* Europe. The pressure of nomadic pastoralism served to define Eastern European history not so much directly but, as Alex Anievas and Kerem Nisancioglu observe (2015), as a result of its "uneven and combined" impact upon the western and eastern parts. Whereas the indigenous evolution of the East was repeatedly retarded by Mongol invasions (Anderson 1974, 227), for Western Europe the unintended consequences were relatively benign. Dutch and English merchants benefited from the *Pax Mongolica*, which also facilitated the diffusion of key technologies of power, such as gunpowder and navigational instruments, from East Asia. In such ways, the Mongol Empire played an epoch-making part in establishing the preconditions for the capitalist development of Western Europe (Anievas and Nisancioglu 2015).

From the sixteenth century, or thereabouts, one can speak of an emergent European identity, in the sense of an identity focused on the idea of a geo-cultural region (Europe) rather than a geo-religious one (Christendom). But the identity shift from Christendom to Europe occurred at precisely the same time as the beginnings of the idea, and the reality, of Western hegemony (Delanty 1995, 47). Consequently, second-class status attached to "Eastern Europe" already at its birth, and this explains its anomalous, hybrid position within the algebra of "orientalization": on the one hand, ever the junior to its western neighbours, chronically "othered" and trailing, whether in technological advance, industrialization or nation building; on the other, part of the "continent" that dominated the world, largely Christian by religion, and boasting a clutch of major dynastic empires – the Habsburgs, Poles and Tsarist Russia. Hence, the contradictory phenomenology of Eastern Europe. In one sense, then, it can appear as a region of "small nations," with histories of being gobbled up by, dominated by, or desperately seeking inclusion within, the various imperial Leviathans that surround them – (Prussia, the Ottoman Empire, the Habsburg Empire, Russia and the European Union) accompanied by the gamut of political responses to that domination: resistance to, accommodation with, or adulation of, the great powers. Yet, at the same time, some of those same imperial powers have themselves been "in" or "of" Eastern Europe. Furthermore, within the region, finer gradations of geopolitical power have been repeatedly created and sustained. Consider post-*Ausgleich* Hungary: a junior partner to Vienna, but itself holding the upper hand over the "small nations," largely Slavic, that came within its borders.

In Western Europe, capitalism evolved comparatively gradually, with the mode of production, class relations, nation-state formation and "consolidated" states developing more or less in parallel, but the formation of a global market dominated by Western businesses and of a world political order controlled by Western states challenged the disparate polities of Eastern Europe to "catch up" or risk subordination. From the vantage point of the Western liberal empires, their system of commercial society represented the pinnacle of human history, entitling them to tutor and boss the "races" who remained idling at a primitive stage of progress. The British Empire, as Uday Mehta has put it (1999, 82), was construed as acting as "an engine that tows societies stalled in their past into contemporary time and history." With this came a novel conception of time, according to which the future holds out the dream of infinite progress, the past is perpetually deficient, and the present "is in constant need of being realigned with the future through the special effort of political intervention" (Mehta 1999, 108). The new, linear understanding of time that evolved in tandem with the rise of capitalism served to justify colonial expansion, for only a world society understood in terms of linear progress achieved by its component countries and regions made development-based comparison possible, with those deemed to be more evolved insisting upon their responsibility to "civilise" the less fortunate. A similar algebra of progress applied within Europe, where, from the eighteenth century onward, the demarcation, invention and positive evaluation of the "West" occurred through its demarcation against the "rest." In the East, beyond the Elbe, the economy was overwhelmingly agrarian, and the ideas of linear time and of progress were slower to emerge.

A case can be made that, Ireland's role vis-à-vis England apart, "Eastern Europe in the eighteenth century provided Western Europe with its first model of underdevelopment" (Larry Wolff, quoted in Bideleux). But this idea – of the East as subordinate to and instructed by the West – arrived slowly and belatedly in the East itself. Only following its own "modernization" did the region finally become "the East." In Russia, notwithstanding the singular project of Peter the Great in the seventeenth century, it was not until the early nineteenth century that the debate between "Westerners" (zapadniki) and "Easterners" (slavophiles) commenced. In other words, the centre-periphery image of East–West relations emerged relatively late, because without the periphery acknowledging and echoing the charge of its relative backwardness, it makes little sense to speak of a model-setting centre.

This is not, of course, to argue that the core-periphery relationship was based simply upon "othering." Prejudice and its internalization were underpinned by imbalances of a political, military and economic kind. These grew markedly in the nineteenth and early twentieth centuries, as evinced most egregiously in Russia's submission to Western and Asian powers in the Crimean War, the Russo-Japanese War of 1905 and the First World War – defeats that, in their turn, catalyzed modernization drives and sparked revolutions. Perceptions of Eastern Europe's inferiority were materially rooted. By almost every relevant index, Segert points out, quoting Rothschild and Wingfield, the region was "less productive, less literate, and less healthy than West Central and Western Europe." Aware of this, modernizing elites modelled institutions and infrastructure on Western examples: Budapest's underground system after London's, Prague's redevelopment of Josefstadt after the Paris of Baron Haussmann, and so on (Berend 1998; Segert 2002). During the Cold War, the narrative of the West as development setter evolved, with an increasing emphasis upon its role as champion of human rights and individual freedom. In the Fukuyaman optic that rose to prevalence as the Eastern Bloc collapsed, the West won the Cold War principally because it represented the most human societal system. It remains the prevailing approach – and, because of it, the 'East' remains incomprehensible.

The explorations in this book of the contemporary identity of Eastern Europe connect directly to a set of debates that concern the academic approach to the study of regions. The form of geographically parcellized scholarship known as area studies has its critics. It tends, they say, to be resistant to innovative methodologies. It is a congeries of disciplines – linguistics, cultural studies, political science and history – heaped together without a theoretical or methodological toolkit to call their own. And in recent years, it has failed to take processes of globalization into account. Area Studies has faced a twofold challenge: the popularity of the "globalization" discourse has rewritten the traditional concept of "area," while the rise of a "new regionalism" and the empowerment of subregional entities have combined to erode the traditional social-scientific assumption that nation states constitute the central actors within geographical regions. Against these criticisms, its defenders – such as Segert, in this book – highlight its encouragement of a discourse free of the boundaries and constraints of the discrete disciplines, enabling perspectives from different disciplinary approaches to be productively combined, and geared to the study of countries other than one's own.

The most trenchant critique of area studies, however, is of the political interests at play. Behind its evolution, Miklóssy points out, lay the knowledge demands of imperialist states. Her chapter discusses the roots of area studies in "the colonial paradigm" whereby powerful states, in their aspiration "to take full advantage of the resources of a distant territory," seek "knowledge of its geography, ethnography, politico-economic systems and culture" – an approach that may appear at face value to be "holistic" but in a superficial and reductive way, with geographical zones drawn to serve as a cultural tag that renders geography homogenous and obscures its history. The apprehension of Eastern Europe in particular, a region conceived of as centring around a threatening Tsarist or Communist Empire, or as a zone of volatility and instability in the interwar period, seemed to require scholarship to be predictive, "problem-solving" (in Robert Cox's terms) and productive of fingertip knowledge that is immediately apprehendable for decision-makers. On similar lines, Bideleux proposes that the persistence within Western academe of the area studies approach to Eastern Europe represents nothing but the consequence of an abiding "orientalism," one that encourages a tendency – doubtless less pronounced among scholars than policy-makers – to lump East Europeans together as a cultural-civilizational "Other." The need therefore is for "a thorough 'de-Orientalization' of (pre)conceptions, perceptions, attitudes and mindsets with regards to 'Eastern Europe' . . . in order to help the inhabitants of post-Communist states to escape or throw off the injurious, essentialist and ethnocentric caricatures and straitjackets which have limited their opportunities and potential for too long." An identifiable Eastern Europe, in Bideleux's view, has ceased to exist, given the end of the Cold War division of Europe and with many Eastern European countries joining Western institutional structures – and boasting faster economic growth rates than their Western neighbours. With the enlargement of the EU, then, has not the study of Eastern Europe lost its *raison d'etre*? The time has surely arrived, he argues, for it to be jettisoned and replaced by European Studies, for the latter has increasingly subjected the study of *all* European societies, "from Galway to Vladivostok, to a single overarching set of conceptual categories, assumptions, approaches and rubrics." This vast zone, according to Bideleux, is inhabited by individuals who are increasingly homogeneous in their "values, priorities and concerns."

Bideleux's appeal for the academic hegemony of European Studies dovetails with his perspective on the EU and its expansion. The EU, in his view, may have taken a regrettable neoliberal turn in its economic policy regime, yet this does not negate its essential nature and its foundational aims: to combat ultranationalism, fascism, genocide and *Machtpolitik*. The countries of East Central Europe that have not yet signed up to its project should therefore "be 'locked into' the EU's supranational civil legal order" – and to the extent that this has not yet occurred, the *Machtpolitik* of Moscow is to blame. These theses are challenged by other contributors to this book. Miklóssy, for example, is concerned that Russia be understood "from within and not from the point of view of Western moral superiority," while Cistelecan chips away at the EU's pacific, solidaristic and antifascist self-image. In Eastern Europe, he argues, "the much dreamed of Western way of life has become a reality only for the select few," and this goes some way towards explaining why, for much of its population, the EU is decreasingly seen as a vehicle of democracy and prosperity. In this context, the recasting of Eastern European political and economic differences as "cultural" serves to justify the failure of decades of EU-steered neoliberal reform to universalize prosperity. Economic differences continue to ensure the maintenance of the subordinate "East," even within Western institutions, with the West cast within the modernizing paradigm in the role of democratizing benefactor, while, in political rhetoric and academic scholarship, power differences are downplayed. Although some scholars asserted that the subsumption of the study of Eastern European societies within European Studies would undermine tendencies to cultural essentialism, such essentialism was instead reconstituted in a new guise, with the new member states conceived of as innately inferior, objects for the Brussels-Luxembourg *mission civilisatrice*. The "main trend of history" (Kornai 2006, 211) was envisioned unidirectionally as the eastward extension of West European institutions and values. Yet, against a backdrop of an increasingly undemocratic EU – witness for example the removal of elected governments in Greece and Italy in 2012 – the master narrative of democratic eastward enlargement loses its lustre. As divisions within the EU widen, for example over attitudes to austerity, refugees, and Russia, what has become of the project to integrate the East? For the contributors to this volume, the challenge is to situate "Eastern Europe" as a whole, with particular reference to its orientalist construction as the other of "the West," while simultaneously analyzing the economic specificities and cultural identities of the various countries of which it is comprised.

References

Anderson, Perry. 1974. *Passages From Antiquity to Feudalism*. London: New Left Books.

Anievas, Alex, and Kerem Nisancioglu. 2015. *How the West Came to Rule: The Geopolitical Origins of Capitalism*. London: Pluto Press.

Berend, Tibor Iván. 1998. *Decades of Crisis: Central and Eastern Europe before World War II*. Berkeley: University of California Press.

Delanty, Gerard. 1995. *Inventing Europe: Idea, Identity, Reality*. Basingstoke: Macmillan.

Kornai, János. 2006. "The Great Transformation of Central and Eastern Europe: Success and Disappointment." *Economics of Transition* 14 (2): 207–244.

Mehta, Uday Singh. 1999. *Liberalism and Empire: A Study in Nineteenth-Century British Liberal Thought*. Chicago: The University of Chicago Press.

Rothschild, Joseph, and Nancy M. Wingfield. 2000. *Return to Diversity. A Political History of East Central Europe Since World War II*. 3rd edition. Oxford: Oxford University Press.

Segert, Dieter. 2002. *Die Grenzen Osteuropas. 1918, 1945, 1989 – Drei Versuche, Im Westen Anzukommen*. New York: Campus Publishers.

The "Orientalization" and "de-Orientalization" of East Central Europe and the Balkan Peninsula

Robert Bideleux

This article first explains how Western "Orientalization" of East Central Europe, the Balkan Peninsula and the Russian Empire during the eighteenth and nineteenth centuries resulted in crude and demeaning "Western" caricatures of "East Europe(ans)". After 1945, such stereotypes were reinforced by the Cold War East–West divide. From the 1980s to 2007, European integration brought about substantial "de-Orientalization" of most of Europe's former communist states. Since 2008, unfortunately, further headway in these directions has been seriously jeopardized by recent "wrong turns", crises and setbacks in the European integration process, above all by the ill-conceived Eurozone project.

1. Introduction

Drawing on Larry Wolff's *The Invention of Eastern Europe* (1994), this article begins by explaining how Western "Orientalization" of East Central Europe, the Balkan Peninsula and the Russian Empire during the eighteenth and nineteenth centuries resulted in crude and demeaning "Western" caricatures of "East Europeans" and helped to polarize modern Europe into "Eastern" and "Western" zones. Western Europe's educated classes increasingly regarded "Eastern Europeans" to be relatively poor, unsophisticated, violence prone and several rungs down the imagined "civilizational hierarchy" — and as occupying positions *intermediate* between the exotic "Oriental despotisms" of Asia and the increasingly bourgeois, "civil", law-governed, regulated, calculating, interest-driven, commercial and open societies of "the West". Since the nineteenth century, stereotyping of this kind has underpinned the dominant Western explanations of (alleged) "East European" susceptibility to serfdom, absolutism, bigotry, xenophobia, anti-Semitism, fascism, communism and related forms of authoritarianism. After 1945, such stereotypes were buttressed by the proliferation of communist regimes and, more ambiguously, by ethnocentric essentializing tendencies within the emerging Western academic field of "East European area studies", which expanded rapidly in the wake of Second World War and the subsequent escalation of the "Cold War". Essentialism "is the idea that humans and human institutions ... are governed by determinate natures that inhere in them in the same way that they are supposed to inhere in the entities of the natural world" (Inden 1990, 2).

Such perspectives highlight the need for further "de-Orientalization" of Western perceptions, preconceptions and attitudes relating to Europe's post-communist states, partly to help their inhabitants to throw off the injurious ethnocentric and essentialist caricatures and constraints which repeatedly have limited their opportunities and potential. This article argues that the gradual widening and deepening of European integration has helped the East Central European and Balkan post-communist states to reap growing benefits from the steadily expanding supranational civil legal order centred on the EU, and that this has been promoting structures, frameworks, opportunities and incentives which offer the most promising ways and means of (i) "de-Orientalizing" these countries; (ii) gradually dissolving or diluting troublesome and divisive primordial attachments and identities; (iii) transcending the essentialist East—West dichotomies which have polarized modern Europe; (iv) diminishing the privileged (and often irksomely arrogant and intrusive) tutelary roles of West European states vis-à-vis Europe's post-communist states; and (v) merging what remains of "East European area studies" into the broader, less-essentialist and less-ethnocentric framework of "European Studies".

Unfortunately, further "deepening" and "widening" of European integration and further "de-Orientalization" of Europe's post-communist states have been seriously impaired by the major economic crises that have afflicted Europe (as well other parts of the world) since 2008. The relatively "easy" credit-financed and consumption-led economic growth, which most European states enjoyed to varying degrees from 2001 or 2002 to 2007 or 2008, has been superseded by a harsher economic climate which has strained social fabrics and cohesion, dampened business confidence, curtailed foreign direct investment (FDI) and impeded further deepening of European economic integration. These setbacks were exacerbated by the Eurozone crisis and austerity measures of 2010—13, which pushed the Czech Republic, Hungary, Slovenia, Croatia, Serbia, Bosnia, Macedonia and Montenegro into "second recessions" in 2012 (IMF 2014, 181, 184). Indeed, most of the Balkan post-communist states have been suffering socio-economic setbacks and hardships even more severe than the more widely publicized ones in the Eurozone's "Southern Periphery". Together with the concurrent growth of European xenophobia, this has been retarding further "de-Orientalization" of the Balkan post-communist states and further "deepening" and "widening" of European integration. Nevertheless, there has been strikingly little reversion to earlier forms of authoritarianism, xenophobia and introversion in the Balkan and East Central European post-communist states. In the face of adversity, most of their inhabitants seem to have gritted their teeth and attempted to work ever harder than before, exhibiting the kind of "work ethic" which the more affluent West used to exhibit but now appears to be shedding. Ethnocentric and essentialist stereotypes are continually being confounded!

For reasons of manageability and space, this article concentrates on East Central Europe and the Balkan Peninsula — albeit with occasional cross references to the Russian Empire, the USSR and the post-Soviet states, where appropriate.

2. The Implications of the "Demi-Orientalization" of East Central Europe, the Balkans and East Slavic Europe

Wolff (1994) has very influentially argued that the modern Western conceptions of "Eastern" and "Western" Europe originated as mental constructs (products of "mental mapping"), and that the "invention" of "Eastern Europe" was crucial to the subsequent "Orientalization" of its inhabitants.

> In the Renaissance the fundamental conceptual division of Europe was between North and South ... It was Western Europe that invented Eastern Europe as its complementary other half in the eighteenth century, the age of Enlightenment. It was also the Enlightenment, with its intellectual centers in Western Europe, that cultivated and appropriated to itself the new notion of "civilization," an eighteenth-century neologism; and civilization discovered its complement, within the same continent, in shadowed lands of backwardness, even barbarism [located in so-called "Eastern Europe"] ... Poland and Russia would be mentally detached from Sweden and Denmark, and associated instead with Hungary and Bohemia, the Balkan lands of Ottoman Europe, and even the Crimea ... The Enlightenment had to invent Western Europe and Eastern Europe together, as complementary concepts, defining each other by opposition and adjacency. (Wolff 1994, 4–5)

> The idea of Eastern Europe was entangled with evolving Orientalism ... There was room for ambiguity. The geographical border between Europe and Asia was not unanimously fixed ... Such uncertainty encouraged the construction of Eastern Europe as a paradox of simultaneous inclusion and exclusion, Europe but not Europe. Eastern Europe defined Western Europe by contrast, as the Orient defined the Occident, but was also made to mediate between Europe and the Orient. One might describe the invention of Eastern Europe as an intellectual project of demi-Orientalization. (Wolff 1994, 7)

The "Orientalization" of Western perceptions of these vast and diverse territories and their very variegated inhabitants was part and parcel of the ways in which the rising Western powers variously constructed or reimagined the world and its inhabitants as a "natural" or Divinely ordained hierarchy of "races", "civilizations", and military and economic powers, as has recently been reaffirmed by Quijano (2008), McCarthy (2009), Mazumdar, Kaiwar, and Labica (2009), Hobson (2012), Seth (2013), and Cannadine (2013), among others.

Within these overarching global hierarchies, the (mostly Slavic) inhabitants of the Tsarist and Habsburg Empires and the Balkan Peninsula were increasingly perceived to be economically, "civilizationally" and racially inferior to "Westerners", albeit superior to the world's non-white peoples (cf. Mälksoo 2009). However, Wolff's thesis that a new East—West polarity simply superseded a hitherto dominant North—South polarity was incomplete. There had been significant older East—West divisions within what became "Europe" and/or "Christendom", notably: (i) the ancient Greeks' famous East—West distinction between the "Oriental despotisms" of "Asia" and a precociously civilized "Europe" centred on the Balkan Peninsula (rather than on Western Europe, which was then at least as "primitive" and "barbaric" as many West Europeans later imagined the Balkans to be!); (ii) the Roman Empire's East—West divide; and (iii) the related East—West division of medieval "Christendom" into a "Latin" West and a "Byzantine"/Orthodox East. Wolff also underplayed the degrees to which Europe retained major North—South divisions. Indeed, his "Eastern Europe" was rapidly subdivided into a Balkan "South" and an East Central European "North". Nevertheless, the Western Enlightenment's "invention of Eastern Europe" was later buttressed by:

(i) the marked "Orientalization" of the Ottoman-dominated parts of the Balkans, which was visually reinforced by the diffusion and growing portrayal of Muslim minarets and bathhouses, Ottoman coffeehouses and flamboyantly exotic "Oriental" dress (as emphasized by Todorova 1997 and Goldsworthy 1998);

(ii) the emergence of an economically and technologically dynamic and geopolitically hegemonic "capitalist world-system" centred on Europe's Atlantic seaboard, in relation to which the economies of East Central Europe, the Balkans and the Tsarist Empire were relegated to the roles of less developed and increasingly subordinate "semi-peripheries", producing and exporting raw or semi-processed primary products in exchange for West European manufactures and financial-cum-commercial services (Wallerstein 1974—89), although this actually occurred more gradually, more endogenously and much later than Wallerstein recognized (McGowan 1981, 2—9; Bideleux and Jeffries 2007b, 91—109, 140—41, 155—90; Bideleux 2010);

(iii) the gradual emergence of a divide between a Western Europe of increasingly mercantile "national" monarchies which had largely dissolved serfdom by the fifteenth century, and an Eastern Europe still dominated by more agrarian multinational empires which maintained either serfdom or similarly "feudal" forms of exploitation up to the nineteenth century (Anderson 1979; Bideleux and Jeffries 2007b, 19—20);

(iv) the post-1947 institutionalisation of a "bipolar" Europe: Comecon (CMEA, 1949), the Warsaw Pact (1955) and the ruling communist parties, as the main institutional pillars of the emerging Soviet bloc; and its Western European counterparts, the first-ever institutionalizations of Western Europe in the form of the OEEC, NATO, the Council of Europe and the European Communities (Bideleux 1996; Bideleux and Jeffries 2007b, 459–488).

The "Orientalization" of Western perceptions of the Tsarist and Austrian Habsburg empires and the Balkans was reinforced by long-standing traditions of dichotomous "binary" thinking and cultural stereotyping (Powell 1999). These developed particularly strongly (albeit not exclusively) in Western Europe and the USA, which increasingly "Orientalized", "lumped together" and "lorded it over" most of the "non-Western world" (Lévy-Bruhl 1926; Said 1978; Mazumdar, Kaiwar, and Labica 2009; McCarthy 2009; Suzuki, Zhang, and Quirk 2014). Especially from the 1820s onwards, these divisions were greatly magnified by massive widening of economic, technological and military disparities between the so-called "civilised" peoples of the West, on the one hand, and non-Western peoples ("the Rest"), on the other (Pomeranz 2002; Bayly 2004; Maddison 2007, 382; Piketty 2014, 60–61). The ensuing cultural stereotypes have long supported a priori cultural determinist explanations of divergent levels and patterns of economic and technological "development" and "performance" as well as divergent political and social outcomes. Influential examples include Max Weber's writings on "the Protestant ethic", "Confucian" China and "Hindu" India (Weber 1930, 1951, 1958) and Arnold Toynbee's study of the rise and decline of "civilizations" (Toynbee 1935–54). Within Europe, Western Christendom (albeit in two distinct variants — Roman Catholic and Protestant) has been widely perceived to be "essentially" different from Orthodox Eastern Christendom. Montesquieu, Adam Smith, François Guizot, Karl Marx and Karl Wittfogel, among others, influentially counterposed the supposedly "linear" development of "Western Europe" or "the West" to the allegedly "cyclical" trajectories and developmental "stasis" of the exotic and despotic "Orient". This dichotomy was later modified slightly by the elaboration and popularization of various hypostatized conceptions of "Asiatic forms of society". These were influentially applied to the Tsarist Empire, not least by Marx, Engels and some of their "Marxist" followers (Melotti 1977, 25–26, 82–87, 134), and to the Ottoman-dominated Balkans (Todorova 1997; Goldsworthy 1998). In addition, influential books by Jaszi (1929), Delaisi (1929), Mitrany (1930, 1951), Tiltman (1934) and Anderson (1979) have postulated similarly *binary* socio-economic counterparts to Europe's alleged East–West cultural divides.

Nevertheless, the ways in which "the West" explained its economic, military and technological dominance over "the Rest" (including Eastern Europe) have often amounted to little more than self-serving exercises in self-justification, self-congratulation, arrogance and complacency (as emphasized by Said 1978, Blaut 1993 and Bessis 2003, among others). These increasingly salient discourses and modes of thinking developed in tandem with the various forms of cultural "Othering" associated with Western colonialism, Orientalism and racism (Said 1978; Breckinbridge and van der Veer 1993; Lockman 2003; McCarthy 2009; Hobson 2012).

Kohn (1944), Sugar (1971), Plamenatz (1973) and Gellner (1994, 115–117), among others, advocated a very influential dichotomy between the (alleged) *innately "ethnic" character of Eastern European nations and nationalisms* and the (alleged) *innately "civil" character of Western European nations and nationalism*. Shils (1957) and Geertz (1963, 108–113) popularized a corresponding distinction between societies and nationalisms based on "primordial" attachments and identities and those based on "civil" ones.

> By a primordial attachment is meant one that stems from the "givens" — or, more precisely, as culture is inevitably involved in such matters, the assumed "givens" — of social existence: immediate contiguity and kin connection mainly, but beyond them the givenness that stems from being born into a particular religious community, speaking a particular language ... and following particular social practices. These congruities of blood, speech, custom and so on, are seen to have an ineffable, and at times overpowering, coerciveness in and of themselves. One is bound to one's kinsman, one's neighbour, one's fellow believer, *ipso facto*; as the result not merely of personal affection, practical necessity, common interest, or incurred obligation, but at least in part by virtue of some unaccountable absolute import attributed to the very tie itself. (Geertz 1963, 109–110)

Europe's more "easterly" nations came to be widely regarded as having age-old identities based primarily on strong *primordial affective* ties and attachments centred on ethnicity, race, religion or kinship, which allegedly fostered strong susceptibilities to (or reliance on) "ethnic collectivism", strong authoritarian rulers, state intervention, public provision, state enterprise and the politics of non-negotiable absolutes (nationalist as well as religious). Conversely, Europe's more westerly nations were increasingly regarded as having age-old identities that were allegedly based upon on more pragmatic and negotiable "civil" ties and rational calculation, including broadly shared commercial "interests", incipient liberal democratic and bourgeois values, and strong attachments to private property, individualism and private enterprise.

The notion of an overarching dichotomy between a Europe of mostly "civic" nation states in the west, and a Europe of mostly "ethnic" nation states further east, acquired *some* substance following the attainment of full "national independence" by the emerging Greek state in the 1830s, by Romania and Serbia in 1878, by Bulgaria in 1908, by Albania in 1912–13, and by Poland, Hungary, Czechoslovakia and the Baltic States in 1918–20, broadly on the basis of the emerging doctrine of "national (ethnic) self-determination", or at least in partial correspondence to ethnic boundaries (Bideleux and Jeffries 2007b, 110–130, 306–343). The resultant "ethnocracies" — states that were regarded as the exclusive property of the majority ethnic group (Crainic 1938) —

increased the disadvantages, structural under-privileging and systemic persecution of ethnic minorities and considerably facilitated the rise of strong ultranationalist and fascist movements in East Central Europe and the Balkans between 1918 and 1945. In combination with the xenophobia and interethnic tensions stoked up by the imposition of unpopular but largely ineffectual "minority protection treaties" and by Nazi Germany's skilful invocation and manipulation of "rights of self-determination" for the substantial German minorities resident in non-Germanic countries (dangerously mimicked by Putin's Russia in 2014), this increasingly jeopardized attempts to build or consolidate liberal forms of capitalism and representative government in inter-war Europe's newest states and contributed to the outbreak of Second World War, widespread ethnic cleansing and mass genocides (Ramet 1997, 2007; Bideleux and Jeffries 2007a, 10–16; Bideleux and Jeffries 2007b, 321–329).

Nevertheless, such distinctions need to be used very cautiously, in order to guard against the dangers of simply introducing additional overstated essentialist dichotomies and stereotypes into a field already littered with unexploded landmines. The long-fashionable dichotomy between the alleged *innately "ethnic"* character of "East European" nations and nationalisms and the alleged *innately "civil"* character of Western European nations and nationalism was greatly exaggerated and oversimplified (Nikolas 2000; Mungiu-Pippidi 2004). It seriously underestimated the large degrees to which (i) "any successful nationalism must necessarily draw upon principles of both civic and ethnic nationalism" (Mungiu-Pippidi 2004, 24); (ii) the nationalisms and social ties which developed in some "easterly" parts of Europe (notably the Polish-Lithuanian Commonwealth and more sporadically the Kingdom of Hungary and the Czech Lands) were more "civil" and "cosmopolitan" than "ethnic", while those that developed in some of Europe's "western fringes" (Ireland, Wales, Scotland, the Basque country, Catalonia) as well as in Belgium, Scandinavia and Germany were decidedly "ethnic"; (iii) Europe's East–West differences were not innate, "civilizational", "essential" or cultural, but transient outcomes or reflections of then-prevailing East–West differences in *socio-economic and state structures*; and thus were not absolute and intractable "givens", but situational, circumstantial and potentially changeable or malleable (Bideleux and Jeffries 2007a, 15–21; Bideleux and Jeffries 2007b, 7–16).

3. The Continued "Orientalization" of Europe's Communist States during the Cold War Heyday of "East European Area Studies"

Although Western "area studies" programmes and centres had some pre-1940s precursors (Szanton 2004, 37, 77–83, 263, 341–342, 352), they mushroomed in response to the exigencies of Second World War and the subsequent intensification of the Cold War (Diamond 1992; Byrnes 1994; Wallerstein 1997; Szanton 2004, 9–13, 20, 37–40, 74–77, 119, and 219–228). The major Western Powers decided that it had become crucial to "know" their Cold War arch enemy, the USSR, to whom they had been allied during Second World War, and its actual or potential affiliates (Horowitz 1967; Diamond 1992; Byrnes 1994; Schiffrin 1997; Szanton 2004, 8–12, 20). The large sums of money which various Western governments and rich private charitable "foundations" then pumped into Russian/Soviet and East European Studies, along with the resultant explosive growth of training, career and research funding opportunities, increased the temptations and inducements to "lump together" actually very diverse "East Europeans" and treat them as "essentially different" from "Westerners", even though they had mostly been forcibly corralled into the "Soviet bloc".

Some analysts even perceived the Soviet bloc's "homo Sovieticus" to be essentially different from (or the antithesis of) the West's "homo economicus", whom the dominant practitioners of the Western social "sciences" (especially economics) increasingly treated as the archetypal rational, secular, utility-maximizing, staunchly individualistic Westerner (Arrow 1951; Downs 1957; Hollis and Nell 1975; Amadae 2003). Such perceptions underpinned the development of Western neoclassical and neoliberal economics and the ascendant "rational actor", "rational choice" and "public choice" conceptualizations of (and approaches to) Western politics (Downs 1957; Buchanan and Tullock 1962; Buchanan and Tollison 1972, 1984; Monroe 1991; Self 1993; Friedman 1996). The disciplinary "mainstreams" of the Western humanities and social sciences tended to assume that Western economic, political and cultural ascendancy rested on the allegedly unique secular rationalism, scientific spirit, pluralism, individualism, tolerance and "moral exceptionalism" of Western societies, and that this fundamentally differentiated the West from "the Rest". (This dichotomy, crudely foreshadowed in works such as Lévy-Bruhl 1926; was trenchantly critiqued in Wilson 1970; Monroe 1991, Self 1993; Friedman 1996 and Gress 1998; but has recently received a sophisticated restatement in Huff 2011).

To be sure, insofar as the USSR, the Balkans and East Central Europe were still regarded as being "European" (and thus only "demi-Orientalized" and "semi-peripheral"), it was widely accepted that they had to varying degrees participated in the development of Western secular rationalism and science. Nevertheless, the collectivism and étatism of "Soviet and East European" political, economic and social systems was widely ascribed to prior experiences of serfdom, state-direction (dirigisme) and protectionism, which differentiated them from the West in various *sui generis* ways. Thus, not always intentionally, the boom in "East European area studies" programmes tended to reinforce (as well as challenge) Cold War-induced "essentialization", stereotyping and exaggeration of alleged cultural or "civilizational" differences between "the West" and Europe's communist states (Bonnell and Breslauer 2004, 218–239; Comiso and Gutierrez 2004).

Homo sovieticus concepts have proven quite durable in Western media perceptions of the USSR and Russia (e.g. "The Long Life of Homo Sovieticus", in *The Economist*, December 10, 2011). However, such concepts have been used much more ironically or satirically within former communist states, most famously in Alexander Zinoviev's novel *Homo Sovieticus* (1986). The underlying cultural determinism and "essentialism" have been subjected to powerful critiques by Ledeneva (1998, 2006), who has shown that the distinctive practices, ties, relationships and networks which emerged in Soviet and post-Soviet Russia, Central Asia, Azerbaijan and Lithuania can be more satisfactorily explained in non-culturalist and non-ethnocentric terms — as *coping strategies* adopted and developed in order to operate and survive in very difficult Soviet and post-Soviet environments, rather than as ethnocentric manifestations of "essentially" Russian, Central Asian, Azerbaijani or Lithuanian culture.

Unfortunately, the rapid expansion of "area studies" in the West after 1945 was not initially accompanied by a commensurate expansion of comparisons between regions. Instead, there was a proliferation of inter-country comparisons within macro-regions (or geopolitical "zones of influence") designated by Westerners. Until the dramatic "rise of the Rest" between the 1980s and the 2000s (complemented by the rise of postcolonialism, multi-regional democratization studies and subaltern studies), "the Rest" were seen through Western, rather than local "conceptual lenses". Area studies "severed regions from one another in the scholarly mind", so they were "almost never studied in relation to one another"; and this narrow focus perpetuated "dichotomies and stereotypes" and fostered "radical separation and opposition", in ways that implied "a neat division of the world into clear and simple zones, each with a fixed place in a [global civilizational] hierarchy. Yet cultures and societies are not abstract, oppositional, static and sealed units that function in isolation, or fit along an evolutionary spectrum from the barbaric to the civilised" (Nader 2010, 84).

4. "Eastern Europe" and "East European Area Studies" after the Cold War

After the Cold War, unfortunately, cultural essentialism and cultural determinism were given fresh leases of life by Samuel Huntington's (in)famous essay (1993) and subsequent book (1996) on "the clash of civilizations". He not only revived the modes of "civilizational" stereotyping popularized by Spengler (1926), Weber (1930, 1951, 1958) and Toynbee (1935—54), but shrewdly combined these with the "clash of civilizations" concept coined by Matthews ([1926] 2006) and popularized by Lewis (1990). Cultural or "culturalist" (pre)determination of economic performance and political outcomes was similarly promoted by Pye (1985), Harrison (1992), Putnam et al. (1993), Fukuyama (1995) and Hofstede (2000) as well as by the influential symposium entitled *Culture Matters* (Harrison and Huntington 2000). (For critiques of these forms of cultural essentialism and determinism, see Ledeneva 1998, 2006; Mungiu-Pippidi and Mindruta 2002; Commisso and Gutierrez 2004; Bideleux 2007, 2009b, 2011.)

THE POLITICS OF EAST EUROPEAN AREA STUDIES

This article is not suggesting that all or even most of the academics involved in "East European area studies" actively supported these trends. Quite the contrary, several major symposia on the development of "area studies" have stressed that most of the academics involved in these fields have been all too aware of the dangers of "essentializing", stereotyping, caricaturing or exaggerating the unity of the macro-region(s) in which they have specialized, and have furnished trenchant warnings on the potential pitfalls of "area studies" (see Breckenridge and van der Veer 1993; Mirsepassi, Basu, and Waever 2003; Szanton 2004; Iskandar and Rustom 2010). Nevertheless, the very existence of "area studies" appeared implicitly to validate presuppositions among politicians, the media and wider publics that the characteristics and/or problems which defined the "areas" studied rested on "essential", distinctive and/or monolithic unities of culture, values, mentalities and attitudes, even though this contradicted the perceptions of many specialists working in each of these fields.

Exaggeration, "essentializing" and caricaturing of Europe's alleged "East–West" differences reached new peaks during the paroxysms of violence in the Western Balkans in 1992–95 and 1998–2001, especially in the media-led "ancient ethnic hatreds" explanations of those conflicts (e.g. Kaplan 1993, 1994; Gerolymatos 2002). Unsurprisingly, such tendencies have peaked again in response to the increasingly menacing authoritarianism of the Putin regime, which has largely been underwritten and made possible by Russia's large windfall gains from high international oil and gas prices, the resultant inflows of FDI and Russia's growing "rentier state" characteristics. These factors greatly increased the Putin regime's wherewithal, freedom of action and relative immunity from democratic challenge, scrutiny and accountability (Bideleux 2009b, 123–31; Bideleux 2011, 343–350).

However, instead of conveniently offloading all "blame" for post-Soviet Russia's colossal failings onto the corrupt and ineffectual Yeltsin regime and the increasingly authoritarian Putin regime, it needs to be recognized that Western states failed to respond as vigorously, generously and constructively as they could (and should) have done to the Gorbachev and Yeltsin regimes' attempts to promote a pan-European "common European home" between c.1988 and c.1995. During that brief period of exceptional instability and flux, liberal-minded and socially responsible Russian parties and movements still had some chance of winning out. This offered various opportunities for an enlightened consortium of Western states to mount a massive "Marshall Plan" to "pump-prime" a much-needed Russian economic reconstruction and faster integration into Western and new pan-European structures, as was cogently advocated at the time by President Vaclav Havel (in *The Financial Times*, May 10, 1992), Professor Jeffrey Sachs (1995), *The Economist* (October 1, 1994, 28) and *The Financial Times* (March 4, 1993, 19; April 5, 1993, 4; and June 20, 1994, 17), among others. Unfortunately, most Western leaders preferred to "play hard ball" with Russia during the 1990s — providing as little economic and technical assistance as they could get away with, thereby bringing Russia to its knees economically and thoroughly marginalizing and humiliating it.

THE POLITICS OF EAST EUROPEAN AREA STUDIES

Cheered on by US general William Odom (1998), the West took full advantage of Russia's prostrate condition in order to implement successive Eastward enlargements of NATO — consciously reneging on the unwritten pledges given to Mikhail Gorbachev in 1990 not to enlarge NATO eastwards (in return for active Soviet cooperation in German reunification and rapid withdrawal of Soviet forces and personnel from East Germany and other former "satellite states"). Instead of using this relatively brief "window of opportunity" to overcome or transcend Europe's "East—West" divide and *Machtpolitik*, all that the West's hard-nosed leaders accomplished during the 1990s was to move Europe's damaging East—West divide slightly further to the East. Even this meagre gain was obtained at an exceedingly high price: not only squandering a possibly unique opportunity to establish a more integrated and inclusive pan-European order, but profoundly alienating and atomizing the millions of Russians who felt deeply humiliated and let down by the West's unrelentingly tight-fisted and myopic parsimony towards an impoverished and temporarily incapacitated post-Soviet Russia during its most desperate hours of need (Cohen 2001, 2009, 141–180; Bideleux 2009b, 130–34). The Western powers thus helped to create and put in place the Putin menace which now poses such serious threats to the peace, stability, integrity and further economic development of several other post-communist states. One almost invariably reaps what one sows.

Unfortunately, with the notable exception of Vaclav Havel, many East Central European intellectuals actively contributed to this deliberate (but ultimately counter-productive) marginalization and cold shouldering of Russia by pursuing a largely successful campaign to "re-brand" their very diverse countries and region as "Central Europe" — a name which Westerners had previously applied primarily to Germany and Austria (Schöpflin 1989). The centrepiece of this campaign was the "Othering" and denigration of the "civilizational" attributes of the predominantly Eastern Orthodox East Slavs (Russians, Ukrainians and Belarussians), South Slavs and Romanians and of the predominantly Muslim Albanians — greatly overstating and "essentializing" the alleged "civilizational" differences. The campaign strongly resembled the ways in which the eastern half of Europe was "civilizationally" downgraded and "Othered" by the West during the eighteenth and nineteenth centuries and again during the Cold War. Sadly, instead of rising above the "dirty tricks" to which their forebears had been subjected by West Europeans in the past, the champions of the new "Central Europe" played a similarly "dirty trick" on their erstwhile East Slav, South Slav, Romanian and Albanian associates in the former "communist bloc". This ploy helped to secure their own prior admission into the EU — ahead of Europe's allegedly "inferior" Eastern Orthodox and Muslim post-Communist states, who were consigned to the back of the queue for EU membership for many years to come. Significantly, most of the literature championing this "Central Europe" barely mentioned the region's key roles in the rise of ultra-nationalism, anti-Semitism, fascism and Nazism, nor its extensive complicity in the Holocaust. This illustrates a pattern of "nested

Orientalism", wherein one nasty Orientalism lurks inside another, like a set of Russian "mamushka" dolls (Bakic-Hayden 1995). (The key texts in this sorry story, above all Kundera (1984), are more fully assessed in Comisso and Gutierrez (2004) and in Bideleux and Jeffries (2007b, 8–22).) This was an early warning that, instead of being decisively renounced and banished, "essentialist" and "Orientalist" (pre)conceptions of "Eastern Europe" would henceforth be deployed more exclusively against South and East Slavs, Romanians and Albanians.

5. Gradual "de-Orientalization" of the East Central Europe and the Balkans since the end of the Cold War

The gradual widening and deepening of European integration has been building or promoting the kinds of structures, frameworks, opportunities and incentives which offer the most promising ways and means of "de-Orientalizing" Europe's post-communist states. These ongoing processes can help these countries gradually to erode, dissolve, dilute and transcend the essentialist dichotomies, ethnocentrism, and primordial attachments and identities which have been the bane of modern Europe, but which have had especially catastrophic impacts on East Central Europe and the Balkans (Snyder 2003, 2010; Bideleux and Jeffries 2007a, 2007b). Indeed, a paramount need in these regions has been "to free human beings from the bondage of ethnic collectivism — that source of all strife and enslaver of human individuality" (Havel 1996, 40).

This has aided the gradual supersession of old-style "East European area studies" by less-essentialist, less-ethnocentric and more broadly-framed "European studies", highlighting the increasingly predominant *commonalities* in European heritage, aspirations, priorities and concerns (Clark 2002; Lee and Bideleux 2009; Mikus 2011). Region-specific specialists and linguists are still needed to deal with certain kinds of region-specific challenges and problems (Comisso and Gutierrez 2004, 269–273, 290), but this is compatible with greatly increased use of Europe-wide categories, criteria and conceptual frameworks. Furthermore, much of this work has been taken over by scholars from the countries in question, thereby greatly reducing the roles of outsiders and of Western "Orientalizing".

A "post-Western Europe" is emerging (Delanty 2003), with broadly convergent aspirations, priorities, mores and concerns (Bideleux 2009b) and increasingly "soft" and permeable internal European borders, although many of Europe's borders still remain much more controlled and controlling than they were before 1914 (Zielonka 2002; Lee and Bideleux 2012, 86–89). The inhabitants of Europe's post-communist states appear to have become just as consumerist, materialistic, secular, agnostic and freedom-loving as their West European counterparts, and the power of "primordial" attachments and identities has diminished all over Europe — not just in Western Europe. Among the findings of the transnational opinion and value surveys conducted across many

European countries during the 1990s and 2000s, what stood out most strongly were not the much-publicized but largely superficial and/or ephemeral East–West differences, but rather the growing similarities in concerns, aspirations, priorities and preferences right across Europe (Miller, White, and Heywood 1998, 28; Rose, Mishler, and Haerpfer 1998; World Bank 2007; Halman and Voicu 2010). "In terms of attitudes to liberal values, the rule of law, tolerance for minorities, multi-party elections, the state's role in the economy, socialist values, nationalism and cultural conformity, there was little to choose between Britain and states emerging out of Tsarist, Ottoman or Habsburg rule. A large majority in all the states surveyed, including Russia, supported liberal and democratic values as well as the institutions embodying those values, and this was reflected in structured voting patterns' (Sakwa 2003, 343–44; cf. Fish 1998, 232–33, 1999, 797–802).

Contrary to frequent claims that the (alleged) preponderance of "ethnic" over "civic" nationalism in Europe's post-communist states would make (or keep) their inhabitants more xenophobic than West Europeans, by the mid-2000s, overall levels of electoral support for xenophobic/ultra-nationalist parties were no higher in Europe's post-communist states than in Western Europe (Mudde 2005, 268–71; Mudde 2007, 2–4). Strikingly, in the May 2014 European Parliament elections, xenophobic/ultra-nationalist parties obtained considerably greater support in most of the participating *West European* states than they did in the participating *post-communist* states (EU 2014; *The Economist*, May 31, 2014, 13, 31). Indeed, the seemingly inexorable resurgence of xenophobia in Western Europe since the 1980s has further challenged "ethnic-civic" East–West dichotomies and complacent claims that West European societies and nationalisms are inherently more "civic" than their more "easterly" counterparts. It also poses the greatest current threats to the liberal and democratic values and institutions on which many Europeans still pride themselves and (rather naively) like to define "Europeanness". The word *resurgence* is used in preference to *rise*, partly as a reminder that modern Europe has long been the major home and progenitor not only of liberal and democratic values, practices and institutions, but also of particularly vicious (often genocidal) forms of colonialism, ultra-nationalism and fascism.

The reasons why Russia and some other European CIS countries remain separated from the rest of Europe have rather more to do with the continuing deeply-entrenched and vice-like grip of the Russian "deep state" on Russia and several of its post-Soviet neighbours, and with Russia's continuing stranglehold on their energy supplies (see Bideleux 2009b, 123–31; Bideleux 2011, 343–350), than with supposedly unbridgeable cultural or "civilizational" differences (Dawisha and Deets 2006). Blaming this situation mainly on cultures, values and attitudes of the inhabitants of these countries in effect offloads the main "blame" onto the current chief victims, thereby letting most of the bigger culprits off the hook. When Ukrainians, Moldovans, Georgians and even some Russians have felt able to speak and vote freely (i.e. without constant fear of surveillance, "dirty tricks" and reprisals), they have often shown that they too would like to emulate the East Central European, Baltic and most Balkan states in developing more liberal forms of representative government and capitalism and closer links with the West. Indeed, despite the continual endeavours of Russia's "deep state" to prevent this, most of Europe's post-Soviet states have been steadily reorientating their economies and societies towards Western "market civilization", partly in endeavours to escape the dead hand of the past and the clutches of Russia's "deep state" (Bowden and Seabrooke 2006; Zahra 2011). Worldwide, *the most potent solvents* of the primordial attachments and identities which perpetuate dysfunctional cultural introversion and seclusion are the seductions emanating from so-called "McDonaldization" and "Coca-colonisation" alias (Western-style) consumerism, hedonism, agnosticism and selfish materialism. Such forces may well be as utterly crass and ignoble as they are often portrayed to be. Yet, insofar as they help to erode, dilute, dissolve, marginalize or defuse primordial codes, values, attachments and identities, they unwittingly help to make the world a less violent, less combative and ultimately safer and more tolerant place.

Since the demise of Europe's communist regimes in 1989–1991, after a roughly 45-year delay imposed by their largely involuntary "imprisonment" within the debilitating and stultifying communist bloc, the East Central European and Balkan post-communist states have belatedly become free to follow/replicate more or less the same trajectories of political and economic liberalization and European integration which West Europeans have pursued since the launching of the OEEC in 1948, the Council of Europe in 1949 and the European Communities during the 1950s. They have been doing this for much the same reasons as West Europeans, in response to broadly similar priorities, interests, aspirations, needs and concerns, and with broadly comparable skills, capabilities and levels of education, despite starting from lower initial levels of economic development, capital stock, technology and economic and institutional infrastructure than the much more fortunate West Europeans (Bideleux and Jeffries 2007b, 556–618). Situational factors, material interests, pragmatism, expediency and ever-shifting structures of opportunity and incentives have played striking roles in the ensuing transformations and reorientations of the East Central European and Balkan post-communist states and the reconstruction of their national and regional alignments and identities during their protracted integration into the structures, policies and practices of the EU (Vachudova 2005, Chs. 6–8; Grzymala-Busse 2007; Bideleux and Jeffries 2007a, 7, 581–591). These far-reaching transformations and reorientations have highlighted the fluidity and malleability of culture(s), attitudes and mindsets, which have mostly responded positively to changing structures of opportunities and incentives (see Dimitrova 2004; Kelley 2006; Pond 2006; Bideleux and Jeffries 2007a; Cohen and Lampe 2011).

So long as Europe's communist regimes and the Soviet bloc survived, many upwardly mobile people tended to see educational and career advantages in "toeing the line" and subscribing to illusory "blood and soil" claims that some of the "imagined" bonds, cultural affinities, empathies or "fellow feelings" among "East Europeans" and "Slavs" were real and made them "essentially" different from West Europeans. After the demise of the communist regimes, however, the swift "westward turn" in perceived educational and career opportunities, advantages and incentives quickly encouraged the ambitious, the upwardly mobile and the young to rapidly readjust their career and life-style orientations and aspirations towards the perceived "richer pickings" offered by the West, the EU, Western-style consumerism and the aptly termed "global standards of market civilization" (Bowden and Seabrooke 2006).

It is similarly prudent to avoid essentializing "Europe" as a whole, and not just its variously conceived constituent regions. Far from having had a fixed "essence" which can plausibly be traced back to antiquity, "Europe" and its constituent regions have repeatedly been kaleidoscopically reinvented and reconfigured (Bideleux 2001, 2003; Pocock 2002; Lee and Bideleux 2009; Passerini 2012). Indeed, "there are no 'pure' identities: 'Europe' or 'the West', and Asia or Africa or the 'non-West', were historically constituted, each defining the other" (Seth 2013, 2). Since the sixteenth century, moreover, (macro-) regional identities have become "real" tangible entities mainly as by-products of successful economic development and economic integration.

> Today's Asia has been shaped by economics, and it is an Asia of increasing prosperity, of interdependence and of global financial influence. This is the first time since the Mongol empire established by Genghis Khan ... that Asia has become truly connected together ... Economics, rather than nomadic horse-men, is the force that is now turning Asia into a coherent entity ... The commercial links that are emerging inside Asia are producing the deepest and most extensive integration that Asia has ever seen. They are bringing about the very creation of Asia. They are, in effect, creating a new continent. (Emmott 2009, 25)

Similarly, Latin America has been integrated by the post-1980s economic liberalization, mounting pan-American trade and investment flows, ICT and the emergence of Mercosur, much more than it ever was by its past Iberian over-lords and cultural heritage (Bideleux 2005). Amongst the Arab states, "What decades of Pan-Arab sentiment had failed to achieve, the (1973–1983) oil boom accomplished effortlessly ... [as] the economies of the capital-scarce labour-exporters and the labour-scarce oil exporters became tightly linked through massive flows of labour and capital across national borders" (Chaudhuri 1997, 1). European integration has repeatedly advanced most strongly during economic upswings, and has either slowed down or gone into reverse during economic downswings (Bideleux 1996, 15–18). This strongly sug-gests that the "Europeanization" of East Central and East European aspirations, attitudes, identities, values, beliefs and priorities has been and will continue to be driven in large part by European economic development and economic integration. Unfortunately, while the economic environment was relatively favourable to this from the early 1990s to 2007 or 2008, it has been far less so since 2008/2009 (as discussed in section 6).

6. The Transformative Impacts of European Integration in the East Central European and Balkan Post-Communist States

Starting in the early and late 1990s, respectively, the East Central European and Balkan post-communist states were in large part "driven to change" by their pursuit of integration into the EU — with the exacting and largely non-negotiable (take-it-or-leave-it) terms and conditions of EU membership acting as particularly powerful pressures, incentives and catalysts for transformation (Dimitrova 2004; Schimmelfennig and Sedelmeier 2005, 9–10, 224–225; Grabbe 2006; Bideleux and Jeffries 2007b, 574–613). This gradually promoted strong cross-party consensuses on macroeconomic policies, neoliberal pro-grammes of economic liberalization and privatization, considerable restructur-ing of institutions and industries, and extensive judicial and legal reform, including promotion and protection of human and minority rights. The rise of more "horizontal" networks and power relations gradually helped to constrain and bring to account the strongly hierarchical, patrimonial and clientelistic "vertical" power structures bequeathed by the communist regimes. Gradual "restructuring" and "structural transformation" gave fairly steadily increasing substance to the rule of law, equality before the law, limited government, media independence and pluralism, more law-governed and pluralist "civil societies", more "level playing fields", "civil economies" (as coined by Rose 1992) and the gradual strengthening and entrenchment of civil liberties and liberal forms of representative government. The major downsides have included greatly increased inequalities of income and wealth and a veritable "counter-revolution" with regard to gender equality (Galligan, Clavero, and Calloni 2007; Ramet 2007; Bideleux 2009a, 2009b, 2009c).

The EU has become the crucial overarching political, economic and legal framework for over half of all Europeans. This is the framework within which most of the rules, laws, institutions and policies governing the conduct of political and economic activity are collectively and consensually negotiated, formulated and upheld. The EU member states have constructed a unique and remarkably robust supranational civil and legal order which (despite its much-publicized "democratic deficits") strongly promotes and protects the rule of law, limited government, civil liberties, human and minority rights, increased gender equality, formal non-discrimination, multiculturalism, minority cul-tures, multi-level governance and (at both national and subnational levels) relatively liberal forms of representative government.

François Duchêne, who served in Jean Monnet's team of close assistants and advisors from 1952 to 1963, repeatedly emphasized that its most transforma-tive achievement was that a vast range of matters previously dealt with by "national" ministries (of foreign affairs, foreign trade, defence, home affairs, justice, finance, education, health and the like), as part of *inter-state relations*, were increasingly being handled *within a single overarching civil institutional policy framework and legal jurisdiction* — i.e. in much the same ways that states deal with purely "domestic" matters. It was in these senses that relations between EC/EU member states had been "domesticated", "tamed", "civilianized" or "made civil" (cf. Duchêne 1994, 369, 404–406; Duchêne 1996, 27–28). This has given all member states (largely irrespective of their size, wealth and power) and their citizens increasingly equal juridical rights, obligations and standing, by placing them a "European civil system" whose rules and laws are applied increasingly equally to all EU states and citizens. Until the 1940s, disputes between the European states had traditionally been resolved by *force majeure*, by flexing of muscles or (in the last resort) by *going to war*. Within the EC/EU framework, by contrast, such disputes were being routinely resolved by *discussion, negotiation and mediation,* which would usually continue for as long it took to reach agreement on (re)solutions which the participating parties could live with. Failing this, they would go not *to war* but *to court* – ultimately to the Court of Justice of the European Communities in Luxembourg or, on matters outside EC/EU jurisdiction, to the European Court of Human Rights in The Hague.

The EC/EU countries have thus constructed – and now work within – a supranational "Kantian" order characterized by ever-increasing emphasis on rule-governed multilateralism, commercial ties, diplomacy, negotiation and cooperation, all of which is structured and undergirded by robust consensually negotiated common frameworks of policy, law, rules, procedures and rule of law. This has almost entirely superseded or displaced the previous Hobbesian environment characterized by inter-state anarchy, unilateralism and "might is right" (*Machtpolitik*) (Kagan 2003, 3–8, 55–75). In crucial respects, *the EU is not merely based upon the rule of law; in essence, it is the rule of law.* This is not merely its chief *raison d'être*, but also its main modus operandi. It has both embodied and greatly contributed to the expansion of "regulatory governance" (Majone et al. 1996) and the "judicialization of governance" (Sweet 2000).

This article's understanding of the transformations wrought by EU membership (and the quest for it) derives primarily from Duchêne's conception of the EC as a novel form of "civil" or "civilian power" (Duchêne 1972, 1973), rather than the concept of "normative power Europe" coined and popularized by Manners (2002), which is often mistakenly treated as a substantial advance on or development of Duchêne's conception. These conceptions are not analogous. Duchêne's is much closer to Zielonka (1998) and Kagan (2003) than to Manners (2002, 2006, 2008). Manners himself has identified six key differences between his "normative power Europe" concept and Duchêne's conception of the EC as a novel form of "civil" or "civilian power" (Manners 2006, 175–177). Unfortunately, Manners has erroneously claimed that Duchêne's "focus, shared with [Hedley] Bull, was invariably the strengthening of international society not civil society. Thus both Duchêne and Bull shared an interest in the maintenance of the status quo in international relations which maintained the centrality of the Westphalian nation–state" (Manners 2002, 238). The exact opposite was the case. Duchêne was passionately committed to radically *transforming* the status quo, rather than *maintaining* it; and to *replacing* the Westphalian state system with a "civil" system, whose fundamental character would be much closer to relations *within* a state than to relations *between* states. That was primarily what he meant by "civil" or "civilian" power, which he also described as "a new stage on political civilisation. The European Community … would have the chance to demonstrate the influence which can be wielded by a large political co-operative formed to exert essentially civilian forms of power" (Duchene 1973, 19).

The Manners concept of "normative power Europe" is more problematic and less useful than Duchêne's conception of the EC as a novel form of "civil" or "civilian" power. Projection of the EU's "normative power" (its capacity to lead "normatively" through its favoured norms, values, precepts and ideas) has mainly been effective when the EU holds or wields sufficient "leverage" to be able to insist on certain conditions being met as preconditions for membership and/or major economic assistance. Prior to EU membership (or much-needed economic support) being placed on the negotiating table, and even more after it is "in the bag", the EU's "normative power" is more easily ignored or resisted. Another limitation of "normative power Europe" is that it reads like a manifesto for a new "mission civilisatrice" — a reincarnation of European colonialism, tutelage and imperialism, with not-so-latent messianic pretensions and potential (Diez 2005, 621—625). The concept is also far too smug, preachy, sanctimonious and self-congratulatory. It rests on unwarranted presuppositions of (Western) Europe's moral and "civilizational" superiority over its Others — and this really gets the Others' backs up.

By contrast, Duchêne's conception of the EC/EU as a form of civil or "civilian power" neither made nor rested upon claims of (West) European moral or "civilizational" superiority (Duchêne 1972, 1973). It simply pinpointed key ways in which European integration had transformed the nature and basis of relations between European states and suggested that other parts of the world could draw useful empirical conclusions from this. The main ways in which the EC/EU has managed to exert enduring transformative influence have usually had much more to do with innovative frameworks, reframing of issues and institutional or systemic entrepreneurship and creativity than with the exercise of "normative power".

The East Central European and Balkan post-communist states had particularly strong needs and incentives to be brought into the common frameworks of law and policy constructed by the EC/EU. Integration into this supranational civil legal order has offered them the greatest scope for bringing about forms of legal and institutional restructuring that are capable of defusing, overcoming or transcending the tensions, grievances, disputes, minority problems, economic problems and geopolitical vulnerabilities that have afflicted these countries far more than any other part of Europe over the past century (and have done so in ways that also dragged them and many millions of other people into two World Wars).

Many of the territorial, size-related, minority-related and economic problems facing the East Central European and Balkan post-communist states can be partially *mitigated* or *alleviated,* but cannot readily be overcome or resolved, within the narrow and restricting confines of the nation state. In these contexts, the nation state framework tends to contribute more to the problems to be solved than to the potential solutions.

A key reason for this is that these states have for the most part remained "ethnocracies": states that are quite tenaciously regarded as "belonging" exclusively to the dominant/titular ethnic group, who can use them in whatever way the duly elected representatives of that group see fit. Democratization per se offers relatively little relief from such problems, not least because it tends to empower ethnocultural majorities (collectivities) much more than ethnocultural minorities (Ramet 1997, 2007, 33–106; Bideleux and Jeffries 2007a, 5–16; Bideleux and Jeffries 2007b, 321–329). The EU supranational civil legal order, by contrast, has created a legal order/framework which has placed states, nations and ethnicities of widely differing size, wealth, strength on increasingly equal legal footings in relation to the ever-widening range of matters that falls under EU jurisdiction. These include rights of movement, consumer rights, environmental rights, racial and gender equality and nondiscrimination, and (above all) the EU's Single Market, which has fostered so-called "level playing fields" in ever-more industries. During the run up to the major "eastward enlargement" of the EU in 2004, the use of a tough combination of "conditionality" and "norms" helped to curb discrimination against ethnic minorities quite substantially (Kelley 2006). The EU also bends over backwards to enable elected or appointed representatives of small states to participate on juridically equal footings with those of big states in EU institutions and in transnational deliberations on EU policies and development. This occurs to degrees unheard of in the "old Europe" of sovereign states, where larger states tended to impose their own interests, agendas and wishes by *force majeure* and ride roughshod over those of small states. The Low Countries and later Ireland and Denmark were the first to reap such benefits, which also have major significance for the states that gained EU membership in 2004, 2007 and 2013, as well as for the current applicants, because most of these are small.

Most of these countries have been too small, poor, weak and undiversified to be able to offer domestic markets and resource bases large and broad enough to allow their main industries to maximize their potential sales, growth, profits and employment in largely autarkic ways. Their development would be severely constricted if they were to remain dominated by local monopolists and "boxed into" their limited "national" markets and resource bases. To maximize their development potential, it is necessary to open up and internationalize relatively poor, weak and undiversified economies as much as possible, and to prioritize specialization and "least-cost" export-led growth (Trotsky 1926, 1928; Cerny 1997; Bideleux 2014, 105–110). Indeed, two of the major lessons that can be drawn from the inter-war economic crises and from the 1947—73 economic boom are that Europe's small economies have tended to be the biggest losers from "beggar-my-neighbour" protectionism and the biggest beneficiaries of open-market regimes. The EU's Single-Market regime goes a long way towards meeting such needs because it has long worked assiduously to establish and maintain "level playing fields" as well as open markets.

The creation of the EU, combined with the imperative to "Europeanize Germany" in order to forestall renewed attempts to "Germanize Europe" (Thomas Mann's refrain in 1953), has engendered an environment in which small nations no longer feel much need to "club together" in often uncomfortable unions intended to counter potential threats from powerful neighbours. For example, Europe's expanding civil order facilitated the Czech-Slovak "velvet divorce" of 1993, since when Czechs and Slovaks have coexisted much less fractiously than they did as co-occupants of a single state.

7. The Marked Slowdown in Economic Growth, Integration and de-Orientalization since 2008, especially in the EU's Balkan "Super-Periphery"

From 2001 to 2007 or 2008, almost all of the East Central European and Balkan post-communist states which have either joined the EU or applied for EU membership enjoyed relatively "easy" consumption-led economic growth, financed by substantial net inflows of Western FDI, banking funds, privatization revenues, remittances and relatively buoyant export markets, despite relatively modest domestic rates of saving and investment (Bideleux 2011, 340—343; Hood 2011, 4—6; Bartlett 2013).

West European allegations that post-communist states (especially Romania, Bulgaria and Hungary) have tended to "backslide" once admitted into the EU have led to the setting of ever-more stringent requirements for future entrants (Rupnik et al. 2007; Rupnik 2010; Willis 2011). Croatia's long-awaited accession to the EU was delayed until July 2013 partly for these reasons, albeit also by a long-standing boundary dispute with Slovenia by the conviction of Ivo Sanader (Croatia's Prime Minister from 2003 to 2009) on charges of involvement in large-scale bribery, and by the severity of Croatia's economic recession since 2009. Not surprisingly, therefore, further admissions of Western Balkan states into the EU appear to have been deferred until the 2020s.

Up to a point, the scale of the blatant foot-dragging, procrastination and misappropriation of EU funds in Romania and Bulgaria, and of high-level corruption in Croatia, can make the raising of the EU's membership requirements seem prudent and even in the long-term best interests of the remaining Balkan candidates. Nevertheless, *there are strong counter-arguments that it is wiser to admit such countries into the EU sooner rather than later*. EU membership does change the structures of opportunity, power, incentives and penalties within which their politicians and entrepreneurs operate (Schimmelfennig and

Sedelmeier 2005, 225). The latter gradually learn that it can be more advantageous to comply with EU rules, laws and norms than to flout them. Many of the more "wayward" East Central European and Balkan politicians have gradually become tamed and "house trained" via the larger rewards and opportunities and the wider arenas opened up by accepting EU policies, priorities, precepts and etiquette. EU membership is an elaborate and fairly effective socialization process.

However, ten years after the watershed 2004 "eastern enlargement" of the EU, the outlook is much bleaker. In the eleven post-communist states that are in the EU and the six that are waiting wearily to be admitted, six years of painful economic austerity, sharply reduced or sometimes negative economic growth, and substantially increased unemployment and inequality have wiped much of the shine off EU membership and neoliberal capitalism. These frameworks are now much less widely regarded as "magic bullets", capable of rapidly overcoming or transcending post-communist woes. The harsher economic environment since 2008–09 has for the time being consigned these countries either to the *weak, vulnerable and slow-growing "periphery"* or to the *very poor, vulnerable and slow-growing "super-periphery"* of a slow-growing EU, with no prospect of quick fixes, miraculous rescues, or rapid returns to easy economic growth.

These countries mostly conduct around 60–70% of their foreign trade with the EU, from which they receive most of their bank funding, FDI and remittances. In addition, Slovenia, Slovakia, Lithuania, Estonia and Latvia have joined the Eurozone, while both Kosovo and Montenegro have unilaterally adopted the euro as their currency, and Bulgaria, Macedonia and Bosnia have tied their currencies to the euro. *Thus many East Central European and Balkan post-communist states have become "Euroized" and are deeply embedded in (and dependent upon) the world's most slowly growing macroeconomic region, which is not the best place to be* (Bideleux 2012; Bartlett 2013; Bartlett and Uvalic 2013). This is likely to severely limit the potential growth and room for manoeuvre of the EU's weakest and most vulnerable affiliates, who actually need as much economic growth and freedom of manoeuvre as they can muster.

The much more stringent and rigid monetary and fiscal rules adopted by the Eurozone at Germany's behest in 2010–11 resemble Friedrich Hayek's vision of a very rigidly rule-governed neoliberal international economic order, in which the major macroeconomic and regulatory decisions and instruments are increasingly removed from (state-level) democratic control, scrutiny and accountability and entrusted to unelected supranational technocrats with extensive top-down monetary and fiscal rule-making and regulatory authority (Hayek 1939; Beck 2013; Blyth 2013). The rules, mechanisms, disciplines and structures of this neoliberal monetary union are in effect reproducing much of the automaticity, rigidity and austerity associated with the Gold (Exchange) Standard, which cruelly prolonged and deepened the devastating economic depressions in inter-war Europe (Kindleberger 1973, 16, 28, 292–306;

Eichengreen 1992, xi–xii, 3–28). The imposition of a similarly damaging trajectory on the Eurozone, largely at German insistence, is in practice *promoting* (rather than *averting*) the kind of "German Europe" that European integration was supposed to avoid (Krugman 2011, 2012a, 2012b; Bideleux 2012; Beck 2013, vii, 2013). The Eurozone has thus established an economic governance regime which, besides being very arduous even for its stronger economies and further increasing the EU's already notorious "democratic deficits" (*The Economist* 2012), can only inflict further austerity, rigidity and socio-economic damage and hardships on the Eurozone's weak "Southern periphery" and (even more damagingly) on the EU's even weaker and poorer Balkan "super-periphery".

The course and results of the May 2014 European Parliament elections confirmed that high proportions of European voters perceive the EU to be too intrusive and prescriptive and encroaching excessively and/or unjustifiably on national state sovereignty and freedom of action (*The Economist*, May 31, 2014, 13, 25–26, 31–35). A strong positive reply to such fears and concerns is that *with the sole major exception of monetary union, all of the EU's common institutional, legal and policy frameworks have in practice enabled the governments and citizens of EU Member States to achieve or deliver far more by acting together ("in concert") than they could by acting separately.* Other things being equal, this factor could conceivably allay or mitigate some of the Eurosceptics' and Europhobes' fears and concerns, some of which are not unwarranted.

Unfortunately, attempts to allay these fears and concerns are being severely constrained by that fact that the EU has committed itself and most of its members to a monetary union which has five potentially fatal problems: (i) it is the one EU institutional-cum-policy framework which seriously restricts and encroaches upon the economic sovereignty and freedom of manoeuvre of its member states in ways that are not only anti-democratic, but also potentially very damaging and impoverishing, not least because it rules out currency devaluation, the most tried-and-tested means of promoting relatively rapid, sure-fire, export-led and employment-led recovery from severe economic disequilibria or crises; (ii) the members of this monetary union have merely met formal economic "convergence criteria" (exchange rates, inflation rate and budgetary criteria), and are far from attaining *real economic convergence* (of underlying levels of productivity, unit labour costs, productivity growth, synchronization of economic cycles and the like); (iii) the Eurozone also lacks the other key elements of an "optimal currency area", such as strong redistributive powers and high levels of labour mobility within and between countries; (iv) the Eurozone has already cost much of Europe dearly in terms of reduced economic growth, fiscal austerity, reduced public provision of key services and infrastructure, and considerably increased poverty and unemployment; (v) the Eurozone's decision-making structures and procedures are very cumbersome and elitist, and fall between two stools by offering neither the stronger executive capabilities of a full-blown federal union, nor the greater decentralization and accountability of a looser intergovernmental confederation (Krugman 2011, 2012a, 2012b; Bideleux 2012; Blyth 2013).

Few international monetary regimes have ever survived for very long. This, combined with the implausibility of any group of countries with low labour mobility and widely differing rates of economic growth, productivity growth and wage growth coexisting with a one-size-fits-all exchange rate for very long, makes it all the more reckless and dangerous to have given monetary union such a central role in the European integration project (Bideleux 2012, 398–405; GartonAsh 2012). This deeply dysfunctional monetary union probably can survive for as long its participants remain willing to keep paying its huge price. Already, however, it has not only seriously reduced economic growth, employment and the potential gains from European integration, but in some countries, it has at times come close to jeopardizing the survival of liberal forms of representative government – and could do so repeatedly. It has inflicted especially large and ongoing human and economic costs on the EU's increasingly depressed, impoverished and indebted "Southern periphery" and on its even poorer and weaker Western Balkan "super-periphery". Hence, even if this highly dysfunctional monetary union were to endure, that would only be a pyrrhic victory: its overall cost has already far exceeded its potential (mostly very uncertain) benefits.

The Eurozone countries' (perverse) determination to persevere with this reckless gamble is already impeding attempts to defuse (let alone overcome) the recent groundswells of Euroscepticism, Europhobia and xenophobia, which were most tellingly expressed in the results of the May 2014 European Parliament elections (EU 2014; *Economist* 2014). This places the huge positive dimensions and achievements of European integration project increasingly at risk, thereby gradually transforming the Eurozone's economic crisis into a much bigger political and legitimacy crisis of the EU as a whole (Bideleux 2012; GartonAsh 2012; Beck 2013).

All of this is extremely bad news for the six Western Balkan states still awaiting EU membership. The Eurozone's crisis and dysfunctionalities have severely damaged their growth, employment, public provision, poverty-reduction, and economic-recovery prospects, thereby pushing the admission of additional Western Balkan states even further down the EU agenda and timetable – probably into the 2020s. The Atlantic economies crisis of 2008–09 and the Eurozone crisis of 2010–13 also plunged three existing EU members (Greece, Bulgaria and Romania) into dire economic straits. Consequently, the economies of the Balkan Peninsula as a whole and their deeper integration into the EU have suffered huge setbacks, from which they could take another decade or two to recover.

Exception for Hungary, the East Central European states are nearly all in much stronger positions than the Balkan states. Nevertheless, the Eurozone crisis and dysfunctionalities have also very adversely affected their economic growth, employment levels and economic recovery as well as further deepening of their integration into the EU. This is most likely to rule out any rapid

THE POLITICS OF EAST EUROPEAN AREA STUDIES

resumption of the buoyant consumption- and FDI-led economic and employment growth which nearly all experienced from 2002 to 2007.

8. The Relative Resilience of East Central Europe since 2008

Far-reaching democratization, economic liberalization, marketization, privatization, restructuring and reform of the legal system were carried out fairly successfully and expeditiously in East Central Europe during the 1990s, assisting the emergence of relatively liberal and robust forms of market economy and representative government in most of the region. (the main misgivings concern Hungary — see below). Most of this region's economies have greatly benefited from their inclusion in the 2004 "eastward enlargement" of the EU and from their close proximity to (and increasingly deep integration into) the strong and dynamic German and Austrian economies, many of whose successful exporting firms have found it expedient either to relocate or outsource/ subcontract much of their production from high-waged and strongly unionized Germany and Austria to relatively low-waged and weakly unionized but well educated, trained and skilled East Central Europe. This helped the economies of the Czech Republic and especially Slovakia and Poland to grow rapidly from 2002 or 2003 to 2007 or 2008. It also shielded them somewhat from the full blast of the major economic crises of 2008—09, centred in five excessively "financialized" Atlantic economies (USA, UK, Ireland, Spain, Iceland) which also suffered burst "property bubbles".

Unfortunately, deep integration with Germany and Austria, which had helped to reduce the negative impact of the Atlantic-centred financial/ economic crisis of 2008—09 on East Central Europe, exposed this region to the full blast of the Eurozone crisis of 2010—13 and helped push the Czech Republic, Hungary and Slovenia into a second recession in 2012 (the first being in 2009). The region's recovery could falter if the (still very shaky) Europe-wide economic recovery expected in 2014—15 were to be choked off by further financial crises and/or strict enforcement of the very rigid fiscal austerity regime adopted by the Eurozone in 2010—11.

The disappointing performance of post-communist Hungary (politically as well as economically) and recent major economic setbacks in Slovenia have indicated that locational advantages, inclusion in the 2004 "eastward enlargement" of the EU, flying starts during the 1990s and "being East Central European" would not automatically guarantee that post-communist political and economic transformation would be accomplished much more successfully in East Central Europe than in the much more troubled Balkan states. There are no culturally or locationally preordained outcomes. Circumstances and how astutely governments or regimes play their hands have mattered more than the quality of the hands that those governments or regimes were dealt.

With regard to Hungary, there has been mounting Western (and some domestic) concern at: (i) how blatantly the Socialist Party leadership lied to the electorate about the dire state of the country's public finances in order to win re-election in 2006; (ii) the degree to which the heavily indebted Hungarian economy has been in the doldrums since 2006; (iii) the disturbingly high levels of support obtained by Hungary's xenophobic right in successive parliamentary, local and European elections since 2006; and (iv) the excessive concentration of power and patronage in the hands of Prime Minister Viktor Orban's nationalist governing coalition since it won a two-thirds parliamentary majority in April 2010 (Rupnik 2012) and again in April 2014.

In 1990, few people would have predicted that, in the long term, deeply divided Poland would decisively outperform Hungary, which appeared to have a strong head start in both political and economic transformation; or that Slovakia, hitherto the overshadowed and discontented underdog, would so strikingly outperform the Czech Republic, which started out with major inherited advantages. However, it would be unwise to ascribe the superior post-communist economic performance of Poland and Slovakia to alleged *innate* qualities or virtues (as against circumstantial factors and structural contexts). During the 1990s, Poland was able to use its strong connections and the large Polish communities in the USA, the UK, France, Germany and Italy to mobilize disproportionately large Western aid and to help get most of the cripplingly large hard currency external debt inherited from its former communist regime written off. Hungary, which had fewer connections and a much smaller diaspora, remained heavily weighed down by an inherited hard currency debt that was even greater than Poland's in per capita terms, while Czechoslovakia's communist regime bequeathed very little debt to the post-communist Czech Republic and Slovakia, which thus began with almost clean slates.

Nevertheless, having closely followed East Central Europe's fluctuating fortunes ever since the "Prague Spring", it has been very pleasing to see a new, dynamic and confident Poland punching so far above its weight as the co-designer and co-constructor of a new "post-Western Europe". Poland has not only revelled in being the only EU country to avoid economic recession in 2009. It has also begun to fulfil Willy Brandt's great wish that "reconciliation of Poles and Germans will someday have the same historical importance as the friendship between Germany and France" (Brandt 1972, 272).

9. Balkan Setbacks since 2009

Unfortunately, the gradual integration of the Balkan post-communist states into EU structures, practices and policy frameworks has persistently been impaired by the degree to which clannish, clientelistic and often semi-criminalized *vertical* power relations and power structures have remained deeply and tenaciously entrenched in these countries, although they are being diluted and eroded by the gradual absorption of these countries into a much broader and richer overarching supranational legal and economic order (Pond 2006;

Bideleux and Jeffries 2007a; Cohen and Lampe 2011, 143–67; Bartlett and Uvalic 2013).

While the media have publicized the magnitude of ongoing socio-economic crises in "peripheral" Eurozone countries (particularly Greece, Spain, Portugal, Cyprus, Italy and Ireland), it is less widely known that the Balkan post-communist states have been suffering even greater socio-economic setbacks and hardships (Bartlett 2013). With the sole exceptions of Albania and Kosovo, all suffered painful economic recessions in 2009, precipitated by the crises of 2008–09 centred on the Atlantic economies. Serbia, Croatia, Bosnia, Montenegro and Macedonia experienced a second ("double dip") recession in 2012, as backwash from the Eurozone crisis of 2010–13. All have suffered substantial cumulative reductions in real incomes, public service expenditures and provisions, and health indicators. They have official adult unemployment rates ranging from 25 to 40% of the workforce, but unemployment among people aged 16–24 exceeds 50% in several countries. In Kosovo, Bosnia and Serbia, well over 50% of young people want to emigrate — compounding the damage that high youth unemployment, "brain drains", reduced services and growing poverty are inflicting on Balkan development potential through loss of skills and work habits, "lost generations", and deepening entrenchment of social exclusion (Bartlett and Prica 2012; Djurovic 2012; Bartlett 2013; Bartlett and Uvalic 2013, 4–6; Kovtun et al. 2014, 19).

These poor, weak and dependent Balkan post-communist states seem set to remain locked into institutional and political-economic frameworks and heavily asymmetric power structures that leave them with very limited room for manoeuvre. Many neoliberals regard such limitations as rigorous and healthy ways of keeping these still young, fragile and supposedly "immature" democracies "on the straight and narrow" — or as prudent constraints and insurance against "wayward" attempts to avoid strict monetary and fiscal discipline. However, it remains to be seen how long these countries will peacefully put up with the neoliberal "iron cages of liberty" (Gamble 1996) in which they are entrapped.

> The rapid economic growth that took place in the super-periphery before the onset of the global economic crisis was based on large inflows of external resources ... This pattern is unlikely to be repeated ... Inevitably, future economic growth will need to be based on more effective use of the region's own resources to a far greater extent than in the recent past, including increased savings and improved human capital. This will require a change in the policy process, focusing less on rent-seeking by local political and economic elites and more promoting of productive entrepreneurship and the stimulation of real competition on domestic markets [in place of privatized local monopolies]. Structural reforms are needed that could underpin renewed economic growth, which is the only way to escape the vicious circle of debt, austerity and [further] recession. The reform of the education systems is especially important to improve human capital resources ... If the economies of the region continue to stagnate, the social situation is likely to deteriorate and social unrest and renewed ethnic conflict may erupt. (Bartlett 2013)

The key question is whether the state needs to take the lead in mobilizing the necessary additional resources and coordinating (and promoting agreement on) the main thrusts of activity, or whether this can be left largely to market forces. Neoliberals naturally push the latter option, but Keynesians and the left have repeatedly questioned whether that would suffice. An intermediate solution, promoting cooperation and partnerships between central and local government and local and foreign private capital, could help to speed up the breaking of bottlenecks and maximize growth by mobilizing local and private capital as well as central and public investment. In the interests of broad cooperation, neoliberals could *temporarily suspend their hostility toward public enterprise and allow pragmatic state investment in infrastructure projects and training and related areas to maximize potential economic growth.*

The longer stagnation persists, the more this would also raise the question of whether EU membership, widespread "Euroization" and extensive economic liberalization and privatization have been more of a hindrance than a help to balkan economic development. Becoming ever-more deeply embedded in the EU, the Euro and wider Western structures no longer promise a guaranteed passage to clear blue water, but instead offer very murky and uncertain prospects. This in turn is likely to further dampen the enthusiasm and alacrity with which rulers and citizens continue to internalize or embed their still relatively new Euro-Western orientations and aspirations.

The particularly bleak medium-term economic outlook for the EU's Balkan "super-periphery" calls into question the economic, social and political desirability and sustainability of their current policies, priorities and projects. It remains to be seen how well and how far marketization, restructuring, economic liberalization and further widening and deepening of European integration can proceed amid alarmingly high levels of youth employment, continual emigration of young talent, much-reduced FDI, slow growth of output and weak exports to depressed West European markets.

Turning briefly to Romania and Bulgaria, Western charges of large-scale misdirection or misappropriation of EU agricultural and/or structural funds and of foot-dragging or procrastination over prosecution of perpetrators of high-level corruption and organized crime have fuelled mounting Western allegations that these two countries were admitted into the EU "prematurely" in 2007. It has even been claimed that Romania's governing elites tricked the EU into admitting a country whose rulers had no intention of mending their incorrigibly corrupt and mendacious ways (Gallagher 2009). To some extent, however, this may be the pot calling the saucepan black. Quasi-Orientalist claims that countries, such as Romania, Bulgaria and Croatia, are vastly out of line with EU norms are not so much mistaken, as examples of Western myopia or double standards. There are no black-and-white contrasts here, but merely different shades of grey — different ways of doing corruption and mendacity, some more subtle or sophisticated than others.

10. Prospects: Further Hardships, Slower "de-Orientalization" and Stalled Integration

Much now depends on whether the Eurozone monetary union survives — and at what cost. This very rigid and vulnerable system can probably continue to be propped up for as long as the relatively vast, rich and strong German economy (one of its very few major beneficiaries) remains willing and able to underwrite it by repeatedly "bank-rolling" its weaker members. Hence, it appears that the Eurozone monetary union can be maintained, albeit only by enforcing levels of fiscal stringency/rigidity/austerity which will continue to retard economic growth, maintain comparatively high levels of unemployment, impose further cutbacks in services and public provisions (especially in education, health care, housing, physical infrastructure and measures to relieve poverty and unemployment), and further impoverish the greatly expanded "reserve armies" of poor and/or unemployed persons in the EU's most vulnerable "peripheries" and "super-peripheries", whose governments now incur punitively high borrowing costs whenever markets lose confidence in their willingness and capacity to "stay the course" (Bartlett and Prica 2012; Bideleux 2012; Bartlett and Uvalic 2013; Blyth 2013).

The economic policies and priorities currently ascendant in the EU, especially the measures and mechanisms deemed necessary to "save the Euro", are currently forcing it to forgo many of the potentially large positive gains obtainable from further deepening and widening of European integration. These large and unnecessary costs mainly stem (as in inter-war Europe) from the poverty, hidebound rigidity and extreme inappropriateness of the currently prevailing economic dogmas (Krugman 2011, 2012a, 2012b; Bideleux 2012; Beck 2013; Blyth 2013).

Remarkably, despite this grim environment and outlook, there have so far been very few formal retreats from liberal forms of representative government and the rule of law in the EU's new and prospective post-communist member states. This is largely attributable to: (i) the *social atomization* brought about by neoliberal capitalism, which has steadily sapped capacities and willingness to organize and sustain mass self-defence, protest and resistance; (ii) the remarkable *stoicism* of populations who, having endured successive waves of economic retrenchment, recession, restructuring and hardship since the 1970s, have become so inured to it that their stock reaction to fresh hardships is to just grit their teeth and endeavour to work even harder than before, doing whatever kinds of paid work they can find — if necessary, by emigrating (Bideleux 2011, 339); and (iii) the ways in which *liberal practices and liberal forms of representative government are being steadily internalized, routinized and embedded into the legal, constitutional and institutional frameworks of over half the European post-communist states*. With a few exceptions (above all Russia and Belarus), all have so far resisted the temptations of much more xenophobic, introverted and authoritarian responses to protracted economic recession, mass unemployment and other great hardships (to which about two-thirds of Europe's states had succumbed by 1938 in response to the protracted socio-economic crises of inter-war Europe). Nevertheless, the largely grim economic outlook still has great potential to foster widespread popular demoralization, anxiety and disaffection and to retard further liberalization, democratization and "de-Orientalization" in these countries and further deepening and widening of European integration. As ever, these problems are being treated with staggering complacency by Western Europe's governing classes, who (instead of changing course) seem intent on steering Europe ever deeper into the Euro-mire which they have so insouciantly promoted.

Disclosure statement

No potential conflict of interest was reported by the author.

References

Amadae, S. M. 2003. *Rationalizing Capitalist Democracy: The Cold War Origins of Rational Choice Liberalism*. Chicago, IL: University of Chicago Press.

Anderson, Perry. 1979. *Lineages of the Absolutist State*. London: Verso.

Arrow, Kenneth. 1951. *Social Choice and Individual Values*. New Haven, CT: Yale University Press.

Bakic-Hayden, Milica. 1995. "Nesting Orientalisms: The Case of Former Yugoslavia." *Slavic Review* 54 (4): 917–931.

Bartlett, Will. 2013. "European Super-Periphery." *Academic Foresights* 7, Jan–Mar. http://www.academic-foresights.com/European_Super-Periphery.html.

Bartlett, Will, and Ivana Prica. 2012. *The Variable Impact of the Global Economic Crisis in South East Europe*, LSEE Papers No. 4. London: LSE European Institute.

Bartlett, Will, and Milica Uvalic, eds. 2013. *The Social Consequences of the Global Economic Crisis in South East Europe*. London: LSE European Institute.

Bayly, C. A. 2004. *The Birth of the Modern World, 1780–1914: Global Connections and Comparisons*. Oxford: Blackwell.

Beck, Ulrich. 2013. *German Europe*. Cambridge: Polity Press.

Bessis, Sophie. 2003. *Western Supremacy: The Triumph of an Idea*. London: Zed Books.

Bideleux, Robert. 1996. "Introduction: European Integration and Disintegration" (1–21) and "The Comecon Experiment" (174–204). In *European Integration and Disintegration: East and West*, edited by Robert Bideleux and Richard Taylor. London: Routledge.

Bideleux, Robert. 2001. "What Does it Mean to be European? The Problems of Constructing a Pan-European Identity." In *Uncertain Europe*, edited by Graham Timmins and Martin Smith, 20–40. London: Routledge.

Bideleux, Robert. 2003. "Europakonzeptionen" ["Conceptions of Europe"]. In *Wieser Enzyklopädie des Europäischen Ostens* [*The Wieser Encyclopedia of Europe's East*], edited by Karl Kaser, vol. 11, 89–111. Klagenfurt: Wieser Verlag.

Bideleux, Robert. 2005. "El Mercosur y la Unión Europea: Cómo se comparan dos modelos de intregración regional?" ["Mercosur and the European union: How Do the Two

Models Compare?"]. In *Economía mundial y desarrollo regional* [*Global Economy and Regional Development*], edited by Raúl Bernal-Meza, 163–183. Buenos Aires: Nuovohacer Grupo Editor Latinoamericano.

Bideleux, Robert. 2007. "'Making Democracy Work' in the Eastern Half of Europe: Explaining and Conceptualising Divergent Trajectories of Post-communist Democratisation." *Perspectives on European Politics and Society* 8 (2): 109–130.

Bideleux, Robert. 2009a. "Post-communist Democratization: Democratic Politics as the Art of the Impossible?" *The Review of Politics* 71 (2): 303–317.

Bideleux, Robert. 2009b. "Rethinking the Eastward Extension of the EU Civil Order and the Nature of Europe's New East-West Divide." *Perspectives on European Politics and Society* 10 (1): 118–136.

Bideleux, Robert. 2009c. "Introduction: Reconstituting Political Order in Europe, West and East." *Perspectives on European Politics and Society* 10 (1): 3–16.

Bideleux, Robert. 2010. "Epilog: Wie sich die Wege von Ost- und Westeuropa trennten" ["Epilogue: The Parting of the Ways Between 'East' and 'West'"]. In *Wieser Enzyklopädie des Europäischen Ostens, Volume 12: Kontinuitäten und Brüche: Lebensformen – Alteingesessene – Zuwanderer von 500 bis 1500* [*The Wieser Encyclopaedia of Europe's East, Volume 12: Continuities and Ruptures: Ways of Life and Migrations from 500 to 1500*], edited by Karl Kaser, Dagmar Gramshammer-Hohl, Jan M. Piskorski, and Elisabeth Vogel, 239–248. Klagenfurt: Wieser Verlag.

Bideleux, Robert. 2011. "Contrasting Responses to the International Economic Crisis of 2008–10 in the 11 CIS Countries and in the 10 Post-Communist EU Member Countries." *Journal of Communist Studies and Transition Politics* 27 (3–4): 338–363.

Bideleux, Robert. 2012. "European Integration: The Rescue of the Nation State?" In *The Oxford Handbook of Postwar European History*, edited by Dan Stone, 379–406. Oxford: Oxford University Press.

Bideleux, Robert. 2014. *Communism and Development*. 2nd ed. Abingdon: Routledge.

Bideleux, Robert, and Ian Jeffries. 2007a. *The Balkans: A Post-Communist History*. London: Routledge.

Bideleux, Robert, and Ian Jeffries. 2007b. *A History of Eastern Europe*. 2nd ed. Abingdon: Routledge.

Blaut, J. M. 1993. *The Colonizer's Model of the World: Geographical Diffusionism and Eurocentric History*. New York: Guildford Press.

Blyth, Mark. 2013. *Austerity: The History of A Dangerous Idea*. New York: Oxford University Press.

Bonnell, Victoria, and George W. Breslauer. 2004. "Soviet and Post-Soviet Area Studies." In *The Politics of Knowledge: Area Studies and the Disciplines*, edited by D. Szanton, 217–261. Berkeley: University of California Press.

Bowden, Brett, and Leonard Seabrooke, eds. 2006. *Global Standards of Market Civilization*. London: Routledge.

Brandt, Willy. 1972. "Willy Brandt: Portrait and Self-Portrait." In *Willy Brandt book*, edited by Klaus Harpprecht, 272. London: Abelard-Schuman.

Breckenridge, Carol A., and Peter van der Veer, eds. 1993. *Orientalism and the Postcolonial Predicament: Perspectives on South Asia*. Philadelphia: University of Pennsylvania Press.

Buchanan, James, and R. D. Tollinson, eds. 1972, 1984. *Theory of Public Choice*. 2 vols. Ann Arbor: University of Michigan Press.

Buchanan, James, and Gordon Tullock. 1962. *The Calculus of Consent: Logical Foundations of Constitutional Democracy*. Ann Arbor: University of Michigan Press.

Byrnes, Robert F. 1994. *A History of Russian and East European Studies in the United States*. Lanham, MD: University Press of America.

Cannadine, David. 2013. *The Undivided Past: History beyond our Differences*. London: Penguin.

Cerny, Philip. 1997. "Paradoxes of the Competition State: The Dynamics of Political Globalization." *Government and Opposition* 32 (2): 251–274.

Chaudhuri, Kiren Aziz. 1997. *The Price of Wealth: Economics and Institutions in the Middle East*. Ithaca, NY: Cornell University Press.

Cohen, Stephen. 2001. *Failed Crusade: America and the Tragedy of Post-Communist Russia*. New York: Norton.

Clark, Terry. 2002. *Beyond Communist Studies: Political Science and the New Democracies of Europe*. Armonk, NY: M. E. Sharpe.

Cohen, Stephen. 2009. *Soviet Fates and Lost Alternatives: From Stalinism to the New Cold War*. New York: Columbia University Press.

Cohen, Lenard, and John Lampe. 2011. *Embracing Democracy in the Western Balkans: From Post-Conflict Struggles toward European Integration*. Baltimore, MD: Johns Hopkins University Press.

Comisso, Ellen, and Brad Gutierrez. 2004. "Eastern Europe or Central Europe?: Exploring a Distinct Regional Identity." In *The Politics of Knowledge: Area Studies and the Disciplines*, edited by David Szanton, 262–313. Berkeley: University of California Press.

Crainic, Nichifor. 1938. "Programmul statului etnocratic" ["Programme of the Ethnocratic State"] in his *Ortodoxie si etnocratie* [*Orthodoxy and Ethnocracy*]. Reissued in 1987. 283–284. Bucharest: Cugetarea.

Dawisha, Karen, and Stephen Deets. 2006. "Political Learning in Post-communist Elections." *East European Politics and Societies* 20 (4): 691–728.

Delaisi, François. 1929. *Les deux Europes* [*The Two Europes*]. Paris: Payot.

Delanty, Gerard. 2003. "The Making of a Post-western Europe: A Civilizational Analysis." *Thesis Eleven* 72: 8–25.

Diamond, Sigmund. 1992. *Compromised Campus: The Collaboration of Universities with the Intelligence Community, 1945–1955*. New York: Oxford University Press.

Diez, Thomas. 2005. "Constructing the Self and Changing Others: Reconsidering 'Normative Power Europe'." *Millennium: Journal of International Studies* 33 (3): 613–636.

Dimitrova, Antoaneta, ed. 2004. *Driven to Change: The European Union's Enlargement Viewed from the East*. Manchester, NH: Manchester University Press.

Djurovic, Katica. 2012. "Youth Unemployment Rates Reaching Epidemic Proportions." *Southeast European Times*, April 23. http://www.setimes.com/cocoon/setimes/xhtml/en_GB/features/setimes/features/2012/04/23/feature-04.

Downs, Anthony. 1957. *An Economic Theory of Democracy*. New York: Harper & Row.

Duchêne, François. 1972. "Europe's Role in World Peace." In *Europe Tomorrow: Sixteen Europeans Look Ahead*, edited by Richard Mayne, 32–37. London: Fontana.

Duchêne, François. 1973. "The European Community and the Uncertainties of Interdependence." In *A Nation Writ Large? Foreign Policy Problems before the European Community*, edited by Max Kohnstamm and Wolfgang Hager, 1–21. London: Macmillan.

Duchêne, François. 1994. *Jean Monnet*. New York: Norton.

Duchêne, François. 1996. "French Motives for European Integration." In *European Integration and Disintegration: East and West*, edited by Robert Bideleux and Richard Taylor, 22–35. London: Routledge.

Eichengreen, Barry. 1992. *Golden Fetters: The Gold Standard and the Great Depression, 1919–1939*. New York: Oxford University Press.

Emmott, Bill. 2009. *Rivals: How the Power Struggle between China, India and Japan Will Shape Our Next Decade*. London: Penguin.

EU. 2014. Official European Parliament Election Results, Brussels: EU. June. http://www.results-elections2014.eu/en/election-results-2014.html.

Fish, M. Steven. 1998. "Democratization's Requisites: The Postcommunist Experience." *Post-Soviet Affairs*, 14 (3): 212–247.

Fish, M. Steven. 1999. "Postcommunist Subversion: Social Science and Democratization in East Europe and Eurasia." *Slavic Review* 58 (4): 794–823.

Friedman, Jeffrey, ed. 1996. *The Rational Choice Controversy: Economic Models of Politics Reconsidered*. New Haven, CT: Yale University Press.

Fukuyama, Francis. 1995. *Trust: The Social Virtues and the Creation of Prosperity*. New York: Free Press.

Gallagher, Tom. 2009. *Romania and the European Union: How the Weak Vanquished the Strong*. Manchester, NH: Manchester University Press.

Galligan, Yvonne, Sara Clavero, and Marina Calloni. 2007. *Gender Politics and Democracy in Post-Socialist Europe*. Opladen: Barbara Budrich.

Gamble, Andrew. 1996. *Hayek: The Iron Cage of Liberty*. Cambridge: Polity Press.

Garton Ash, Timothy. 2012. "The Crisis of Europe: How the Union Came Together and Why it's Falling Apart." *Foreign Affairs* 91 (5): 2–15.

Geertz, Clifford, ed. 1963. *Old Societies and New States*. New York: Free Press.

Gellner, Ernest. 1994. *Nations and Nationalism*. Oxford: Blackwell.

Gerolymatos, Andre. 2002. *The Balkan Wars*. New York: Basic Books.

Goldsworthy, Vesna. 1998. *Inventing Ruritania*. New Haven, CT: Yale University Press.

Grabbe, Heather. 2006. *The EU's Transformative Power: Europeanization through Conditionality in Central and Eastern Europe*. Basingstoke: Palgrave Macmillan.

Gress, David. 1998. *From Plato to NATO: The Idea of the West and Its Opponents*. New York: Free Press.

Grzymala-Busse, Anna. 2007. *Rebuilding Leviathan: Party Competition and State Exploitation in Post-Communist Democracies*. Cambridge: Cambridge University Press.

Halman, Loek, and Malina Voicu, eds. 2010. *Mapping Value Orientations in Central and Eastern Europe*. Leiden: Brill.

Harrison, Lawrence. 1992. *Who Prospers? How Cultural Values Shape Economic and Political Success*. New York: Basic Books.

Harrison, Lawrence, and Samuel Huntington. 2000. *Culture Matters: How Values Shape Human Progress*. New York: Basic Books.

Havel, Vaclav. 1996. "The Hope for Europe." *New York Review of Books*, June 20. 38–41.

Hayek, Friedrich. 1939. "The Economic Conditions of Inter-State Federation." *New Commonwealth Quarterly* Sep. 5: 131–149.

Hobson, John M. 2012. *The Eurocentric Conception of World Politics: Western International Theory, 1760–2010*. Cambridge: Cambridge University Press.

Hofstede, Geert. 2000. *Culture's Consequences: Comparing Values, Behaviors, Institutions and Organizations*. London: Sage.

Hollis, Martin, and Edward J. Nell. 1975. *Rational Economic Man: A Philosophical Critique of Neo-Classical Economics*. Cambridge: Cambridge University Press.

Hood, Ron, ed. 2011. *South East Europe: Regular Economic Report*. Washington DC: World Bank. November 15.

Horowitz, Irving Louis. 1967. *The Rise Fall Project Camelot*. Cambridge, MA: MIT Press.

Huff, Toby E. 2011. *Intellectual Curiosity and the Scientific Revolution: A Global Perspective*. Cambridge: Cambridge University Press.

Huntington, Samuel. 1993. "The Clash of Civilizations?" *Foreign Affairs* 72 (3): 22–49.

Huntington, Samuel. 1996. *The Clash of Civilizations and the Remaking of World Order*. New York: Simon & Schuster.

IMF. 2014. *World Economic Outlook*, April 2014. Washington, DC: IMF.

Inden, Ronald. 1990. *Imagining India*. Oxford: Blackwell.

Iskandar, Adel, and Hakem Rustom, eds. 2010. *Edward Said: A Legacy of Emancipation and Representation*. Berkeley: University of California Press.

Jaszi, Oscar. 1929. *The Dissolution of the Habsburg Monarchy*. Chicago, IL: Chicago University Press.

Kagan, Robert. 2002. "Power and Weakness." *Policy Review* 113 Jun–Jul: 3–28.

Kagan, Robert. 2003. *Paradise & Power: America and Europe in the New World Order*. London: Atlantic Books.

Kaplan, Robert D. 1993. *Balkan Ghosts: A Journey through History*. New York: St. Martin's Press.

Kaplan, Robert D. 1994. "The Coming Anarchy." *Atlantic Monthly*, February 1.

Kelley, Judith. 2006. *Ethnic Politics in Europe: The Power of Norms and Incentives*. Princeton, NJ: Princeton University Press.

Kindleberger, Charles. 1973. *The World in Depression, 1929–1939*. London: Allen Lane/ Penguin.

Kohn, Hans. 1944. *The Idea of Nationalism*. New York: Macmillan.

Kovtun, Dmitriy, Alexis Mayer Cirkel, Zuzana Murgasova, Dustin Smith, and Suchanan Tambunlertchai. 2014. "Boosting Job Growth in the Western Balkans." IMF Working Paper WP/14/16. Washington, DC: IMF. January.

Krugman, Paul. 2011. "Can Europe Be Saved?" *New York Times*, January 12. http://www.nytimes.com/2011/01/16/magazine/16Europe-t.html?pagewanted=all&_r=0.

Krugman, Paul. 2012a. *End this Depression NOW!* New York: Norton.

Krugman, Paul. 2012b. "Europe's Economic Suicide." *New York Times*, April 15. http://www.nytimes.com/2012/04/16/opinion/krugman-europes-economic-suicide.html?_r=1.

Kundera, Milan. 1984. "The Tragedy of Central Europe." *New York Review of Books* April 26. 31 (7): 33–38.

Ledeneva, Alena. 1998. *Russia's Economy of Favours*. Cambridge: Cambridge University Press.

Ledeneva, Alena. 2006. *How Russia Really Works*. Ithaca, NY: Cornell University Press.

Lee, Catherine, and Robert Bideleux. 2009. "'Europe': What Kind of Idea?" *The European Legacy* 14 (2): 163–176.

Lee, Catherine, and Robert Bideleux. 2012. "East, West and the Return of the Central: Borders Drawn and Redrawn." In *The Oxford Handbook of Postwar European History*, edited by Dan Stone, 79–98. Oxford: Oxford University Press.

Lévy-Bruhl, Lucien. 1926. *How Natives Think*. London: Unwin.

Lewis, Bernard. 1990. "The Roots of Muslim Rage." *The Atlantic Monthly* 266 (3): 47–60. http://pages.pomona.edu/~vis04747/h124/readings/Lewis_roots_of_muslim_rage.pdf.

Lockman, Zachary. 2003. *Contending Visions of the Middle East: The History and Politics of Orientalism*. Cambridge: Cambridge University Press.

Maddison, Angus. 2007. *Contours of the World Economy, 1–2030 AD*. Oxford: Oxford University Press.

Majone, Giandomenico, Robert Baldwin, Pio Baake, Fabrice Demarigny, Lluís Cases, Michelle Everson, Laraine Laudati, et al. 1996. *Regulating Europe*. London: Routledge.

Mälksoo, Maria. 2009. *The Politics of Becoming European: A Study of Polish and Baltic Post-Cold War Security Imaginaries*. Abingdon: Routledge.

Manners, Ian. 2002. "Normative Power Europe: A Contradiction in Terms?" *Journal of Common Market Studies* 40 (2): 235–258.

Manners, Ian. 2006. "The European Union as a Normative Power: A Response to Thomas Diez." *Millennium: Journal of International Studies* 35 (1): 167–180.

Manners, Ian. 2008. "The Normative Ethics of the European Union." *International Affairs* 84 (1): 45–60.

Matthews, Basil J. [1926] 2006. *Young Islam on Trek: A Study in the Clash of Civilizations*. New York: Friendship Press.

Mazumdar, Sucheta, Vasant Kaiwar, and Thierry Labica, eds. 2009. *From Orientalism to Postcolonialism: Asia, Europe and the Lineages of Difference*. Abingdon: Routledge.

McCarthy, Thomas. 2009. *Race, Empire and the Idea of Human Development*. Cambridge: Cambridge University Press.

McGowan, Bruce. 1981. *Economic Life in the Ottoman Empire: Taxation, Trade and the Struggle for Land, 1600–1800*. Cambridge: Cambridge University Press.

Melotti, Umberto. 1977. *Marx and the Third World*. London: Macmillan.

Mikus, Marek. 2011. "'State Pride': Politics of LGBT Rights and Democratisation in 'European Serbia'." *East European Politics and Societies* 25 (4): 834–851.

Miller, William, Stephen White, and Paul Heywood. 1998. *Values and Political Change in Postcommunist Europe*. Basingstoke: Macmillan.

Mirsepassi, Ali, Amritsa Basu, and Frederick Weaver, eds. 2003. *Localizing Knowledge in a Globalizing World: Recasting the Area Studies Debate*. Syracuse, NY: Syracuse University Press.

Mitrany, David. 1930. *Land and the Peasant in Romania*. London: Oxford University Press.

Mitrany, David. 1951. *Marx against the Peasant*. Chapel Hill: University of North Carolina Press.

Monroe, Kristen R., ed. 1991. *The Economic Approach to Politics*, New York: HarperCollins.

Mudde, Cas, ed. 2005. *Racist Extremism in Central and Eastern Europe*. London: Routledge.

Mudde, Cas. 2007. *Populist Radical Right Parties in Europe*. Cambridge: Cambridge University Press.

Mungiu-Pippidi, Alina. 2004. "Sense and Prejudice in the Study of Ethnic Conflict: Beyond System Paradigms in Research and Theory." In *Nationalism After Communism: Lessons Learned*, edited by Alina Mungiu-Pippidi and Ivan Krastev, 13–39. Budapest: Central European University Press.

Mungiu-Pippidi, Alina, and Denisa Mindruta. 2002. "Was Huntington Right? Testing Cultural Legacies and the Civilization Border." *International Politics* 39 (Jun.): 193–213.

Nader, Laura. 2010. "Side by Side: The Other is not Mute." In *Edward Said: A Legacy of Emancipation and Representation*, edited by Adel Iskandar and Hakem Rustom, 72–85. Berkeley: University of California Press

Nikolas, Margareta M. 2000. *The Nationalism Project: False Opposites in Nationalism*. Madison, WI: The Nationalism Project.

Odom, William. 1998. "Russia's Several Seats at the Table." *International Affairs* 74 (4): 809–822.

Passerini, Luisa. 2012. "Europe and its Others: Is There a European Identity?" In *The Oxford Handbook of Postwar European History*, edited by Dan Stone, 120–138. Oxford: Oxford University Press.

Piketty, Thomas. 2014. *Capital in the Twenty-First Century*. Cambridge, MA: Harvard University Press.

Plamenatz, John. 1973. "Two Types of Nationalism." In *Nationalism: The Evolution of an Idea*, edited by Eugene Kamenka, 23–26. Canberra: Australian National University Press. London: Edward Arnold, 1976.

Pocock, J. G. A. 2002. "Some Europes and their History." In *The Idea of Europe: From Antiquity to the European Union*, edited by Anthony Pagden, 55–71. Cambridge: Cambridge University Press.

Pomeranz, Kenneth. 2002. *The Great Divergence: China, Europe and the Making of the Modern World Economy*. Princeton, NJ: Princeton University Press.

Pond, Elisabeth. 2006. *Endgame in the Balkans*. Washington: Brookings Institution.

Powell, Timothy B., ed. 1999. *Beyond the Binary: Reconstructing Identity in a Multicultural Context*. New Brunswick: Rutgers University Press.

Putnam, Robert D., Robert Leonardi, and Raffaella Y. Nanetti. 1993. *Making Democracy Work*. New Jersey: Princeton University Press.

Pye, Lucian. 1985. *Asian Power and Politics: The Cultural Dimensions of Authority.* Cambridge, MA: The Belknap Press.

Quijano, Aníbal. 2008. "Coloniality of Power, Eurocentrism and Social Classification." In *Coloniality at Large: Latin America and the Postcolonial Debate*, edited by Mabel Moraña, Enrique Dussel, and Carlos Jáuregui, 181–224. Durham, NC: Duke University Press.

Ramet, Sabrina P. 1997. *Whose Democracy? Nationalism, Religion and the Doctrine of Collective Rights in Post-1989 Eastern Europe.* Lanham: Rowman & Littlefield.

Ramet, Sabrina P. 2007. *The Liberal Project and the Transformation of Democracy: The Case of East Central Europe.* Austin: Texas A&M University Press.

Rose, Richard. 1992. "Toward a Civil Economy." *Journal of Democracy* 3 (2): 13–26.

Rose, Richard, William Mishler, and Christian Haerpfer. 1998. *Democracy and its Alternatives: Understanding Post-Communist Societies.* Cambridge: Polity Press.

Rupnik, Jacques. 2010. "Twenty Years of Postcommunism. In Search of a New Model." *Journal of Democracy* 21 (1): 105–112.

Rupnik, Jacques. 2012. "Hungary's Illiberal Turn: How Things Went Wrong." *Journal of Democracy* 23 (3): 132–137.

Rupnik, Jacques. 2007. "Is East-Central Europe Backsliding?" *Journal of Democracy* 18 (4): 17–63.

Sachs, Jeffrey. 1995. "Consolidating Capitalism." *Foreign Policy* 98: 50–64.

Said, Edward. 1978. *Orientalism: Western Conceptions of the Orient.* London: Routledge & Kegan Paul. (+ London: Penguin, 1985, 1995 and 2003).

Sakwa, Richard. 2003. *Russian Politics and Society.* 3rd ed. London: Routledge.

Schiffrin, André, ed. 1997. *The Cold War and the University: Toward an Intellectual History of the Postwar Years.* New York: The New Press.

Schimmelfennig, Frank, and Ulrich Sedelmeier, eds. 2005. *The Europeanization of Central and Eastern Europe.* Ithaca, NY: Cornell University Press.

Schöpflin, George, and Wood, Nancy, eds. 1989. In *Search of Central Europe.* Totowa, NJ: Barnes & Noble.

Self, Peter. 1993. *Government by the Market?: The Politics of Public Choice.* Basingstoke: Palgrave Macmillan.

Seth, Sanjay, ed. 2013. *Postcolonial Theory and International Relations.* Abingdon: Routledge.

Shils, Edward. 1957. "Primordial, Personal, Sacred and Civil Ties: Some Particular Observations on the Relationships of Sociological Research and Theory." *The British Journal of Sociology* 8 (2): 130–145.

Snyder, Timothy. 2003. *The Reconstruction of Nations: Poland, Ukraine, Lithuania, Belarus, 1569–1999.* New Haven, CT: Yale University Press.

Snyder, Timothy. 2010. *Bloodlands: Europe between Hitler and Stalin.* London: Bodley Head.

Spengler, Oswald. 1926. *The Decline of the West.* London: Allen & Unwin.

Sweet, Alec. 2000. *Governing with Judges.* Oxford: Oxford University Press.

Sugar, Peter. 1971. "Introduction." In *Nationalism in Eastern Europe*, edited by Peter Sugar, and Ivo Lederer, 1–12. Seattle, WA: University of Washington Press.

Suzuki, Shogo, Jongjin Zhang, and Joel Quirk, eds. 2014. *International Orders in the Early Modern World.* Abingdon: Routledge.

Szanton, David, ed. 2004. *The Politics of Knowledge: Area Studies and the Disciplines.* Berkeley: University of California Press.

The Economist. 2011. "The Long Life of Homo Sovieticus". *The Economist*, December 10. http://www.economist.com/node/21541444.

The Economist. 2012. "The Euro Crisis: An Ever-deeper Democratic Deficit." *The Economist*, May 26. http://www.economist.com/node/21555927.

THE POLITICS OF EAST EUROPEAN AREA STUDIES

The Economist. 2014. "Europe's Elections: The Eurosceptic Union." *The Economist*, May 31. http://www.economist.com/news/europe/21603034-impact-rise-anti-establishment-parties-europe-and-abroad-eurosceptic-union.

Tiltman, Henry. 1934. *Peasant Europe*. London: Jarrolds.

Todorova, Maria. 1997. *Imagining the Balkans*. New York: Oxford University Press.

Toynbee, Arnold. 1935–54. *A Study of History*, 10 vols. London: Oxford University Press.

Trotsky, Leon. 1926. *Toward Socialism or Capitalism?*. New York: International.

Trotsky, Leon. 1928. *The Real Situation in Russia*. New York: International.

Vachudova, Milada. 2005. *Europe Undivided: Democracy, Leverage & Integration after Communism*. Oxford: Oxford University Press.

Wallerstein, Immanuel. 1974–89. *The Modern World-System*, 3 vols. New York: Academic Press.

Wallerstein, Immanuel. 1997. "The Unintended Consequences of Postwar Area Studies." In *The Cold War and the University: Toward an Intellectual History of the Postwar Years*, edited by André Schiffrin, 195–211. New York: The New Press.

Weber, Max. 1930. *The Protestant Ethic and the Spirit of Capitalism*. London: HarperCollins.

Weber, Max. 1951. *The Religion of China*. New York: Free Press.

Weber, Max. 1958. *The Religion of India*. New York: Free Press.

Willis, Andrew. 2011. "EU may Impose Monitoring System on Candidate Croatia." euobserver.com. Accessed May 24, 2011. http://euobserver.com/9/32381/?rk=1

Wilson, Bryan R., ed. 1970. *Rationality*. Oxford: Blackwell.

Wolff, Larry. 1994. *Inventing Eastern Europe: The Map of Civilization on the Mind of the Enlightenment*. Stanford: Stanford University Press.

World Bank. 2007. *Salient Findings of the Life in Transition Survey: Europe and Central Asia Region*. Washington, DC: World Bank.

Zahra, Tara. 2011. "Going West." *East European Politics and Societies* 25 (4): 785–791.

Zielonka, Jan. 1998. *Explaining Euro-Paralysis: Why Europe is Unable to Act in International Politics*. Basingstoke: Macmillan.

Zielonka, Jan, ed. 2002. *Europe Unbound: Enlarging and Reshaping the Boundaries of the European Union*. Routledge: London.

Zinoviev, Alexander. 1986. *Homo Sovieticus*. New York: Atlantic Monthly.

From Region to Culture, from Culture to Class

Alex Cistelecan

The paper articulates a sort of dialectic of the ruling culturalist discourse that is currently cast on the East European region. The opening moment analyses the culturalization of the Eastern region's identity and its impact on the continental map. The second stage will shift the perspective to the particular level of the Eastern region itself, where an account of the events surrounding the Romanian "coup d'e´tat" from the summer of 2012 will track down the effects of the culturalist discourse in the internal social dynamic of the region, and its gradual overlapping with the class divide. Finally, once the issue of class is touched, the very adventures of the culturalist discourse will take us back to the transnational level, where the culturalist discourse could overcome the structural issue of class struggle.

The contemporary trick of the rulers is "culture". (G.M. Tamas)

Perhaps not surprisingly, together with its historical and geopolitical relevance, Eastern Europe seems to have also lost much of its specificity. From all perspectives, the region is now nothing but a shadow of the menacing other that it stood for during the cold war: institutionally included — or on the path of being included — in the big Europe, economically on the right capitalist track, politically designed on the universal model of liberal democracies and ideologically the most enthusiastic pupil of the ruling post-ideological discourse. Even in academia, the still unquestioned division of labour — which requires that non-Westerners specialize in their own identity or region because direct experience is, apparently, their only ability, while Western scholars because of their exclusive ability to conceptualize, are allowed to freely roam the earth in the balloon of theory — makes it as if the normal relation appears in reversed form: it is no longer the crucial relevance of the topic that requires scores of specialized scholars; it is rather the constant production of scholars coming from the region that seems to require inventing a specific object of study for them.

And yet, some specific particularities still seem to characterize the region. Even if politically and economically, it is integrated into the European family, the region still lags behind "old Europe", and significant parts of it are not even showing signs of "catching up" with the West in the near future. Overall, the much dreamed Western way of life has become a reality, in Eastern Europe, only for the selected few, while for the rest of the population, the old bleak realities of state socialism regimes now appear rather as the distant dream. But how can one name this specificity, this material difference that persists in spite of all the integration at the formal and institutional level? A name, an explanation had to be found for it: it was culture.

In what follows, I will attempt to critically analyse the mechanism and consequences of applying such a culturalist reading to the Eastern European region. While, by culturalism, I simply mean here, the spontaneous yet systematic translation of social, economic and political factors into cultural terms and values, the choice of deploying such an interpretative tool is far from being neutral and harmless. The tactical advantages of such a culturalist reading are not difficult to guess: firstly, the culturalist explanation has all the appearances of a profound and insightful approach. It discards the merely historical and conjectural pierces through the surface of the deceiving appearances, and reaches through the underlying hidden essence. In this respect, there is no longer any opposition between culture and nature: culture is rather the contemporary, fragmentary mode of appearance of human nature, when there is no longer any universal human nature that could support a grand narrative of progress and emancipation. Conversely, the ironic fate of the concept of human nature can be read in the contemporary notion of cultural differences: what was discarded in the idea of human nature was not its essentialist and unhistorical vein, but merely its progressive potential, which constituted the basis for natural and universal rights. While culture has, in the culturalist discourse, the same nature-like appearance of immutability as human nature, this second nature that virtually discards the first is no longer the ground for universal and egalitarian emancipation, but on the contrary, rather is the presumed explanation for the impossibility — unnatural nature — of such a goal.

Secondly, the apologetic bias of the culturalist discourse is aptly couched in the critical form that this discourse shares even with Marxism. While both approaches share the same attempt to go beyond mere appearances, the way they do it stands in complete opposition. Marxism proceeds from the abstract and "unhistorical" elements that roam at the surface of economic phenomena (money, profit, labour) in order to relate them to the underlying structural causality pertaining to the concrete social relations. In contrast, the culturalist approach starts from the concrete social structures, which are explained by means of their abstract and unhistorical cultural ingredients.

Thirdly, the culturalist insight is not only profound and insightful, and even critical in its form of appearance. It is also "value-free" and allegedly resisting moralization: if it certainly passes judgments and evaluations, it surely does not assign guilt or responsibility. Things are just what they are — and there is not much one can do about it. Overall then, the culturalist approach, in explaining the historical and conjunctural via the unhistorical and the unchanging while also allowing an impartial setting of hierarchies without discrimination or blame, has proved to be the best ideological weapon in making some sense out of the present continental mess.

In this essay, the critical analysis of the culturalist reading follows a somewhat dialectical path. The opening moment consists of tracking down the culturalization of the region's identity and its impact on the continental map, namely the gradual expansion — as revealed by the crisis — of the presumed frontiers of an alleged "Balkan" culture. The second stage will shift the perspective from the continental level, with its opposing cultures of efficiency and competitiveness vs. laziness, passivity and corruption, to the particular level of the Eastern region itself. Here, an account of the events surrounding the Romanian "coup d'état" from the summer of 2012 will track down the effects of the culturalist discourse in the internal social dynamic of the region, and its gradual overlapping with the class divide. Finally, with the article's engagement with class issues, the very adventures of the culturalist discourse will take us back to the transnational level. Here, it is precisely the generalization and radicalization of the culturalist discourse that point towards its possible overcoming and dissolution in the structural issue of class struggle. Hence, at least at the formal level, the present approach is as Hegelian as it gets: from the general, continental level, to the particular, regional moment, and ending with the "universal", structural and transnational apotheosis.[1] Overall then, the essay is not so much — or not only — about the contemporary specificity of Eastern Europe as seen through the lenses and functioning of the culturalist discourse, but rather the other way around: about the political effects and ideological mechanism of the culturalist framing — as instantiated in the Eastern European region.[2]

West European Culturalism as a Systemic Norm of the European Project

The end of the cold war and the European integration of parts of Eastern Europe have relegated the latter from the prestigious status of a politically and historically radical other to that of a mere cultural oddity. The old classification of the three worlds has been thoroughly rearranged. As Pletsch states (quoted in Chari and Verdery 2009, 18), it used to be that the division between the first and the second world had to do with the issue of freedom, whereas both worlds enjoyed, more or less, the same degree of modernity, or were representing different versions of modernity. In contrast, the opposition between the first and the third world was the opposition between modernity and tradition. Now, these two oppositions seem to be conflated in the identity of the Eastern region: the reason why Eastern Europe lags behind the West in terms of freedom is because it lags behind in terms of modernity.

After 1989, instead of progressing towards more freedom, on the basis of its already modern social structure, Eastern Europe seems to have been regressing towards pre-modernity (which is not that inaccurate, considering the effects of the economic integration of the region — in this respect, Frank's (1992) early prediction of the inevitable "Third World-ization" of the region has proved to be right). The political and economic differences are thus recast as cultural differences. According to the discourse prevailing in the official spheres of politics, confirmed by the diagnostic of various scholars and popularized by the dedicated efforts of the media, Eastern Europe is characterized by an innate culture of unfreedom, which explains why, in spite of the excellent advice received from the West, and even in spite of the enthusiastic embrace of the shock therapy of liberal democracy that the local population certainly displayed, integration did not succeed as it should have. A culture of unfreedom, or better still, a culture of corruption still prevails: not the occasional free rider kind of corruption, present in all modern societies, but a sort of massive, pervasive and irreducible culture of corruption. Through this notion of corruption, the culturalization of the region's differences is complete, and its mystification is absolute. Corruption, and even more so when it is elevated to the level of a regional culture, is the conceptual device by means of which the structural and historical specificity of Eastern Europe is explained as unexplainable, as the natural and unhistorical identity of the region.[3] Here, the two axes of the good old three world scheme intersect: we have unfreedom because we don't have modernity; we don't have modernity because we have unfreedom. Corruption explains everything.

However, this cultural turn in the discourse on the region is not an isolated phenomenon. There is a strong culturalist vein in all the recent official discourses of the European elites. This has to do with the contemporary economic crisis and the utter failure of the policies implemented in order to overcome it. In such times of crisis, culture always comes to the rescue. This is what explains the shift from a discourse and set of policies that conceived of European integration merely in institutionalist or procedural terms, to an almost anthropological obsession with the cultural resistance of the region to be integrated.[4]

Formerly, it was thought that a ready-made set of formal rules and a minimalist democratic design would eventually end up generating their own adequate democratic content, thus gradually changing the regional culture into a genuine civic culture of freedom and responsibility. Nowadays, this belief in the material efficacy of the democratic formal framework is abandoned, and it is argued that, on the contrary, the undemocratic culture of corruption that pervades the region is not only untouched by the European acquis communautaire, but also that it even manages to corrupt the democratic design that was so magnanimously exported to the Eastern area. If there is one thing we are supposed to learn from the European crisis — the continental elites seem to say — it is not that the political economy of the EU was wrong from the beginning, increasing internal inequalities and relegating the Eastern regions merely to the status of plantation economies. It is, perhaps, that the dream of integration was too naïve, since it did not pay sufficient attention to the continental cultural differences. These local cultures have proved to be stronger than the project of neoliberal integration: instead of being reduced to their proper place and dimension, as mere folkloric relics for the tourists' amusement, they have swept through politics and economy and corrupted even the best intentions.

But this, apparently, is no longer specific only to Eastern Europe. The same culturalist explanation of the failures of anti-crisis policies is mobilized in relation to Southern Europe.[5] Actually, as long as the Eastern countries did not step out of the neoliberal line, as with Orban's attack on the autonomy of the Hungarian Central Bank, or the alleged Romanian *coup d'état* in the summer of 2012 (more on this below), their enthusiasm in adopting the harshest austerity measures was given as an example to the more reluctant Southern states. In this case, Eastern Europe was again playing the role of promising "New Europe" in which it has been previously cast by Donald Rumsfeld, leading and showing the way to the more inert "Old Europe". In some respects, Eastern Europe still plays this role. Witness, for example, the map of the European countries' votes on the issue of granting Palestine UN membership.

But with regard to the EU-led politics of austerity, things do not run so smoothly anymore in the East. This is evidenced by the large protests that have swept through Hungary, Romania and Bulgaria in the last few years. And almost in this incendiary context, culture is summoned back as the ultimate explanation. When numbers and ratings are tumbling down, unstoppably and yet incomprehensibly, metaphors of cultural insight at least provide the appearance of some sense. When Merkel, Sarkozy and Cameron all proclaimed the death of multiculturalism, this was not because the success of integration has made cultural differences irrelevant, but on the contrary, because cultural differences appear now as insurmountable.

The enthusiastic neoliberalism that pushed through the effort of European integration took a hit from the crisis, triggering retreats into a more sceptical conservatism for which cultural differences are all that matter. But this conservative withdrawal is merely a tactical retreat for a more efficient offensive: the neoliberal project has not been abandoned; it is merely strengthened with a cultural awareness. In this new context, the East of Europe, which until the crisis was in danger of falling into irrelevance, just as much as it was supposed to fall in line with the Western normalcy, assumes a new importance. Its cultural pedigree, which until recently was being viewed as merely a secondary detail, a local charm incapable of hindering the European integration, is reified again and singled out as the main obstacle to the Western system's encounter with its ideal image: the Balkanic corruption and laziness, the Hungarian fascist authoritarianism, the Romanian mendacity, even when true, are falsified in the Western discourse as just so many causes of its own capitalist crisis (Fourcade et al. 2013). That this cultural identity is now in danger of engulfing even the failing Southern States — which, perhaps not incidentally, have changed their titulature from the moralizing "PIGS" to the more anthropological "GIPSI" — is nothing but a proof of its contagious nature. The Evil Empire might be dead, but its cultural pedigree of corruption and unfreedom is still advancing westwards, in more insidious and surreptitious forms than ever.

What all this suggests is that the contemporary European crisis has presumably revealed the latent cultural divisions that cut across the continent. The European culture of efficient and responsible democracy splits the continent into phony and genuine Europeans, with the same acuity and cold objectivity as the recurrent diagnostics of the rating agencies. In this context, it is no coincidence that even the most sophisticated and technical accounts of the present economic crisis seem to point towards a cultural explanation: the permanent surpluses of the German economy are allegedly related to the superior efficiency and productivity of the German workers.[6] But efficiency and productivity are just as much economic notions as they are cultural and moral categories. The solution to the crisis is, then, not so much bailing out the failing peripheral states. After all, the various experiences in Greece, Portugal or Spain have already made it clear that all this amounts to is "sending good money after bad". What is needed instead is a necessary infusion of some "protestant spirit of capitalism" in the periphery (Blyth 2013). In the same way in which, for Adorno, radical materialism discovers theology at its closing point, the final lesson of contemporary political economy, in spite of all its opacity in terms of intuitive meaning, seems to be a reappraisal of the simplest morality and of the most reified cultural clichés.[7]

In this context, Eastern Europe, or, under its more terrifying name, the Balkans, appear to haunt more and more parts of the old continent, revealing their divergence from the European cultural ideal. Or, if we are to put it perhaps a little better, and trace this dynamic exchange of culturizing glances at the continental level, one could say that, in this splitting of the continent along cultural lines, Eastern Europe had a much bigger contribution than one might have expected. After all, the enthusiasm for the good old idea of Europe was resurrected from its neoliberal depression precisely by the "glorious revolutions" of 1989 and by the passion for freedom expressed by the ex-communist societies (Buden 2009; Zizek 2001). Nowadays, this idea of Europe is divorced from the very people that brought it back to life only proves that history doesn't keep track of copyrights. In any case, the external, spatial cultural division of the continent, between true European societies (outperforming everybody in terms of productivity and democracy) and shaky middle formations (be it Mediterranean or Balkan) is, from this perspective, a projection of the internal, temporal division in Eastern Europe, between the European ideal that it brought back to life in 1989, and the reality to which

THE POLITICS OF EAST EUROPEAN AREA STUDIES

Western Europe relegated it afterwards. The presumed path of transition from Eastern Europe to proper Europe has turned into the ever-growing divergence between Eastern Europe's noble ideal of Europe and Europe's ever more sceptical idea of its Eastern periphery.

Tracing Culturalism at the Local Level

Let us now shift our attention from the continental plane to the regional one and trace the effects of this culturalist discourse on the social dynamic of the Eastern countries. In the internalization of the culturalist discourse, the external, continental opposition between different degrees of European culture is projected onto the class divisions of the Eastern societies. In brief, this culturalizing discourse produces a societal split in Eastern Europe, whereby it covers the political issues and the economic inequalities with a cultural narrative which in turn conceals the former and legitimizes their effects.

Perhaps, a short report of the events surrounding the alleged Romanian *coup d'état* from the summer of 2012 will highlight better the mechanism of this culturalizing discourse. It all started with the anti-austerity protests in January and February 2012, which were sparked by the declared plan of the Presidency to privatize the ambulance service. The trigger was not only the plan per se, but also the brutality with which the President dismissed the head of the emergency service: the job was done live on national television and in reaction to this civil servant's doubts about the details and timing of this plan. The political effect of the one-month long protests was a government reshuffle following the weakening of the ruling party by desertions that depleted its ranks of MPs.

The new government, consisting of members of the former opposition (the USL — Social Liberal Union) did not waste time once in power. They quickly removed various high dignitaries such as the presidents of both houses of the parliament and also such figures as the People's Advocate and the director of the Romanian Cultural Institute. All of these had been known for their loyalty to the president. Next, the new government proceeded towards the impeachment of the president: first by suspending him, for having breached the constitution, and then by calling for a referendum, as required by law. The legal validity of these moves has been a subject of heated debate. The president's supporters blamed their opponents for having orchestrated an authentic *coup d'état*, while the other side claimed that their actions did not breach the laws of the land and that if they did, it was only because they had been hasty and impulsive, as required by an extreme situation.

The fact is that these actions had pushed indeed a bit the letter of the law — however, they were perfectly in line with the actions taken by President Băsescu when he had come to power: it has become a tradition in Romania to change all the heads of the administration, once a new party came to power. Faced with this situation the EU intervened. Numerous voices, from the

THE POLITICS OF EAST EUROPEAN AREA STUDIES

political elite (from Barroso to Merkel) up to the leading opinion makers in the European journals, quickly lump together the Romanian political developments with the authoritarian and anti-democratic trend of Viktor Orban, and blamed the rampant culture of greed and corruption affecting Romanian politics.

The vehemence of the EU's intrusion was a surprise for almost anybody following the events from inside the country. No argument was spared, from the culturalizing claim that the events clearly showed the lack of democratic and civic spirit in the region, to the more technical one that these developments would definitely end up by scaring the markets and the investors. The external, democratizing pressure paid its price and led to the imposition of a quorum of 50% for the referendum. It was clear for everybody that this quorum was almost impossible to reach, given not only the usual low political participation of Romanians, but also the approaching summer vacation. The president's strategy radically changed once the imposition of the quorum was achieved: while previously boasting that he would take the fight and win the democratic battle on the field, once the quorum was imposed, he advised his supporters to stay at home.

To complicate matters even further, the census of the population completed almost one year before it had not yielded complete results. The referendum had to go on with incomplete data from several years before, even though everybody knew that the actual population was considerably smaller due to massive emigration. In this context, the result of the referendum was politically crystal clear, albeit legally irrelevant: almost 90% voting for the removal of the president. The turnout was much bigger than expected, but the quorum was missed by a few percentage points. As a result, the president returned to power, even though seven million people voted against him, while only five million had elected him three years before. Democracy was restored and the markets allegedly calmed down. The later publication of the census results in the summer of 2013 further embittered this democratic pill, by showing that the quorum for the referendum had actually been reached.

What interests us here is not only the culturalist discourse surrounding these events, but also its social and political efficacy. In no time at all, social and political issues were translated by leading politicians and journalists in both West and East into a sort of war of civilizations and cultures. The thrust for political power of the opposition and the social anti-austerity agenda of the protesters have been read, both by the president's camp and by the European leadership, as a clash between a very feeble — in terms of support — yet courageous drive towards democracy, personalized by president Băsescu, and a rampant culture of corruption, authoritarianism and populism. To be sure, this cultural reading did not come out of the blue. The very austerity measures — large-scale privatizations, drastic wage cuts in the public sector, etc. — have been from the beginning couched in cultural and civilizational terms, as a painful but necessary attempt to reform and modernize the state. The economic crisis was thus merely a fortunate pretext for this necessary Europeanization of the country.

50

THE POLITICS OF EAST EUROPEAN AREA STUDIES

In this context, the anti-austerity protests and, later, the attempt to oust the president has been presented as a manifestation of society's resistance to this necessary and civilizing effort, as a proof of its still underlying culture of passivity and corruption. Extremely relevant in the mechanism of this cultural reading is the mutual reinforcing and exchange of confirming glances between European leaders and opinion makers, and the corresponding local discourse. Whenever it wanted a further confirmation of the antidemocratic, populist and authoritarian bias of the opposition, the president's camp simply pointed to the allegedly impartial reading of the whole situation in various major European newspapers.

However, the authors of these articles (in *Le Monde, FAZ, Spiegel*) were usually Romanian correspondents who, as even a glance at their texts makes clear, were either misinformed, biased or plain stupid. Nevertheless, the fact that their voice was coming from Europe put their comments beyond any doubt, and further put to shame the opposition's attempt. The fact that the European establishment, through its political leadership and opinion makers, was so heavily involved in — or as they put it, "concerned" at —internal developments further highlighted the cultural and civilizational stakes of the political battle, by turning the whole issue into a pro or against Europe and democracy. On the other hand, the president's political and ideological strategy fitted perfectly with this kind of reading. As a matter of fact, from the very beginning of his terms in office, the president's strategy focused not so much on building his electoral base and mechanisms (he ended up by dumping his own party), but rather on occupying those key places of power that are beyond the electoral game — namely the judicial apparatus, from the constitutional court, to the Anti-Corruption National Department up to the magistrates' ranks. His power was the power of justice and integrity; hence any attack on it would be read as an affront to justice and proof of corruption. From this position, even the electoral game could pass as undemocratic, when its results threaten to change the established justice system. This image of a more and more encircled president, who has only justice on his side, clearly touched the sensibility of the European leaders, which was anyway already informed by its cultural stereotypes. It is only in this way that one can explain the utter naivety of such political leaders as Merkel or Barroso, who seemed to assume that once in power, the opposition would actually change the austerity drive, or at least sweeten it a bit — as indeed it claimed. Obviously, this belief has been contradicted by every political decision that the former opposition took once it occupied the government.

The lasting effect of these political developments and, more importantly, of their phrasing in cultural terms, has been a massive increase in euro-scepticism in Romanian society — a society that until recently was one of the most euro-enthusiastic. Up to now, the overwhelming misery (briefly alleviated only for a few years before the crisis, thanks to the credit boom) was sold to the public as being caused not by integration into European structures and global capitalism, but, on the contrary, by local resistance and deviation from this predetermined path: that is, by the local culture of corruption. Hence, the solution to the devastating effects of global and continental integration was more integrating, more liberalizing reforms, more privatizations, more flexibility. This pill was not so difficult to swallow for a society that, like all the others in the region, but in a much more aggressive way, due to Ceausescu's own way of dealing with the crisis of external debt (Ban 2012), has been used to being treated with uninterrupted austerity ever since the early 1980s. However, the performance of the EU's leadership in the context of the referendum, its obvious bias and patronizing contempt for the anti-austerity message of the population has finally turned things around. The culturalizing and patronizing official discourses eventually produced its perverse effects: if any demand for some kind of social and economic justice is deemed anti-European, then anti-Europeanism must be the way to reach those social desiderata. Thus, for most of the population, Europe is no longer associated with democracy, which eventually has to lead to some kind of prosperity. It appears, instead, more and more as the obstacle to such goals. In this way, the very radicalization and crystallization of the culturalist approach have led it to coincide with the class oppositions traversing Romanian society. The cultural clash at the level of discourse and policies is, now more than ever, the distorted mode of appearance of the underlying class struggle. Thus, even though, the culturalist reading is utterly mystifying, the opposing social camps that it identifies are actually correct.[8]

On the one hand, we have the winners of transition, which roughly correspond to what Eyal, Szelenyi, and Townsley (1998) have labelled *Bildungs burgertum*, i.e. the intellectual and technocratic strata united in the camp of "civil society". Their social status, economic positions, and political ideology are all fused together in the cultural Europeanist mission and identified that they assume. If there were still any doubts, the contemporary economic crisis has functioned at least as a catalyst towards the clarification of their mission and identity; if in the beginning the discourse of "civil society" could pass as an ambiguous third way, between capitalism and state socialism, the crisis has made it clear that the necessary culture of an active civil society translates economically into pure monetarism and austerity. This slippage was, after all, already potentially present in the DNA of the anti-political and anti-communist movement of "civil society". As Eyal, Szelenyi, and Townsley (1998) rightly point out:

> The political dimension of the monetarist ideology has strong elective affinities with the critique of state socialism developed by the dissidents: the ideology of "civil society". This critique problematizes responsibility and initiative in much the same way that utopian monetarism aims to inculcate them through financial discipline. (91)

However, it was the current economic crisis and the austerity measures that finally drove this point home: the discourse of "civil society" revealed its apologetic strain and class bias, which becomes efficient precisely by means of the cultural mystification that it operates. It used to be that the reasoning of the civil society proponents would pass from the necessary political liberties to their necessary material base, the economic freedoms.

Nowadays, the path is reversed: as a leading economist at the Romanian National Bank argued in the context of the referendum, in times of crisis, political freedom — which technically allows for the social grievances of the population to be politically expressed and, eventually, addressed — runs the risk of falling into populism and thus eroding economic freedom (Croitoru 2012).[9] Which means that, in times of crisis, even the culture of democracy can become a dangerous culture of corruption. The alliance of the upper strata of the technocratic milieus with the public intellectuals has never been stronger: while the former complain about the corrupting and dangerous effects of political democracy, the latter carries out the cultural mystification, and legitimates the austerity measures as a necessary anti-communist, Europeanist and civilizing effort (Rogozanu 2014). In this cultural mystification that sustains its concrete, social and political efficiency, the discourse of civil society finally shows its real face, as capitalism's project of perpetual peace, the class dream of a society without classes. Unfortunately, of course, sometimes perpetual social peace needs an economic total war, and the accomplishment of a civil society without classes, comprised only of responsible petit bourgeois and efficient individuals, stumbles on the resistance of the very society it wants to dissolve. But that is just the burden of civilization.

On the other side of the class division, the effects of the culturalizing hegemonic discourse already show their dangerous potential. After all, the main danger of the culturalist discourse is not that it is wrong and mystifying, but that, by means of its own material effects, it might become true. Since the EU is seen as bearing the main responsibility for the country's social misery — in large part, as we have seen, thanks to the role it played in the referendum — the grievances of the population are more and more couched in anti-colonialist and nationalist terms. Hence, instead of an opposition to capitalism and to its increasingly obvious dynamics which relegate the country to the status of a regional periphery based on an economy of extraction and dependent on the influx of foreign capital, we get an opposition that lumps together the critique of the EU and Europeanism together with the critique of modernity, technology or civil rights for minorities which are seen as the immediate cultural and civilizational supplements of this "imperialistic" integration.

The obvious trade-off practiced by the EU when it sweetens the austerity pill with the granting of rights for sexual minorities, for example, further strengthens this kind of reading of events. Even on the timid and barely nascent local Left, the most vocal camps advocate either a necessary divorce from modernity and a return to the traditions of communal farming (vaguely in line with the *décroissance* movement), or a necessary alliance with the religious communities and the traditional resistance to modernity of the Orthodox Church. This is in spite of the fact that the Romanian Orthodox Church has no social doctrine whatsoever and has been accommodating to any kind of political regime, be it socialist or capitalist. Where the economic crisis had at least the welcome effect of crystallizing and revealing the underlying capitalist dynamic, the cultural discourse comes to the rescue and shifts the blame from capitalism to homosexuals, immigrants, modern technology or the corrupted and sold-out elite. Thus, in its generalization and radicalization, the culturalist reading combines the highest social accuracy and transparency with the uttermost opacity and mystification. In other words, the class struggle is finally acknowledged as a menacing haunting spectre in official political discourse, yet its political potential is curtailed precisely by its mystification in cultural terms.

From Local to Structural: Traversing the Cultural Veil

We are now in a position to attempt a differentiation between culturalism as discussed here and the phenomenon of "orientalizm", as a somehow similar ideological tool of the colonial relation. Briefly stated, the difference consists of the fact that the culturalist discourse is at the same time less and more than the phenomenon of "orientalism": on the one hand, it is less constrained and overdetermined by the political and economic system of domination presumed by the colonial relation, since at least on the surface — at the level of superstructure — the periphery is apparently integrated in its case on a more independent and equal footing. And yet, on the other hand, and precisely because of this difference in determinacy at the level of the political and economic structure, culturalism sometimes — and especially in times of crisis — has to be more assertive, aggressive and sharp than orientalism. No wonder that, while orientalism as an ideological vehicle of colonialism always had its "positive", more paternalistic double — in which the colonized other is praised as the stereotype of the good, noble, savage — culturalism as a vehicle of integration into a system of capitalist dependency, at least in its EU version never had — or at least quickly lost — this kind of more sympathetic and paternalistic view of its Eastern internal other. By the time of the first wave of Eastern expansion of the EU, Kusturica was already out of vogue, and the Eastern neighbour started to be seen more in the various stripes of the *classe dangereuse*.

Which leads us to the other significant difference between culturalism as discussed here and orientalism as colonial ideological instrument: while orientalism can, and has inadvertently and in spite of itself led to or contributed to the formation of a movement of resistance and emancipatory political projects in the colony — through the appropriation of the Orientalizing myths by the colony —, the political effect of culturalism, at least in its European display, is less nationally reflected and more class refracted: that is, it leads less to the formation of a movement of common resistance to EU (or German) dependency, and rather to the establishment and deepening of objective, even if it is not yet necessarily self-conscious, transnational class alliances, fractures and relations.

As it appears today on the continental political and media stage, culturalism is the form of expression of the inter-cultural solidarity of the ruling class. Witness the uncanny, yet ultimately revealing, similarity between the culturalist discourses of the neoliberal and neoconservative Western elites on the phenomenon of Eastern European immigration and, generally, on the issue of Eastern Europe's backwardness, and the culturalist discourses of the local, East European, neoliberal and neoconservative elites on the very same people — who just happen to be the immense reserve army of their working class co-nationals, who have become superfluous and uprooted because of the very process of European integration pushed for by their elites (Tamás 2014). From Barroso to Basescu, from Farage to his Eastern avatars, the same exhortations to the liberating effect of overwork and austerity, the same ode to the culture of meritocracy elevated into social Darwinism proper, and, finally, the same attempt to cover the social and economic European depression with culturalist mystifications of the ongoing, and unfortunately, until now, uni-directional, class offensive.

Hence, perhaps this very development, generalization and crystallization of the culturalist discourse could point the way towards its possible overcoming. Once the cultural issue no longer translates into a neat opposition between the undemocratic culture of Eastern Europe (now contaminating also Southern Europe) and the democratic culture of the West, once it corresponds to the very class division, it transcends the regional oppositions and specificities and cuts through all European societies. In this context, Eastern Europe — as a specific region — is again dissolved into a larger entity; but it is no longer the great European family or the global neoliberal project; instead, it stands for the cultural form of appearance of the structural and transnational issue of class struggle.

In the present context, we are no longer dealing with the culturalization of a region, but with the culturalization of class. There are already signs that this cultural war no longer opposes the West to the East, but is being imported even in the once booming and performing Western societies. Even in the West, the increasing pressure on wages and social rights, the wave of privatizations and flexibilizations are sold to their victims as a necessary civilizational effort, as a painful but mandatory divorce from the inertias of the old and rusty social-democratic Europe. You do not want to become like the Greeks, nor do you want to be outbid by Chinese competitiveness. Hence, for the sake of tomorrow, give up your social rights today. This generalization and radicalization of the culturalist discourse thus paradoxically may end up creating or reinventing a sort of transnational working class culture in the very act of demonizing it, and in the absence of any internationalist working class consciousness. Whether the bearers of this demonized culture will become conscious of their transnational objective alliance, whether this recreation of working class culture will lead to a proper international class consciousness and consequent mobilization are hard to tell. What is certain is that this culturalizing approach, even in its radicalized and internationalized form, separates just as much as it unites, mystifies just as much as it illuminates. Its overcoming and re-translation into the structural, historical and transnational issue of class struggle — towards which it is actually already pointing — would be a necessary first step.

Disclosure statement

No potential conflict of interest was reported by the author.

Notes

1. Since the writing of this essay, significant events have been unfolded in Eastern Europe, that, on the one hand, seem to contradict the recent irrelevance of the region in world politics as it is claimed here, and on the other hand largely overshadow the significance and repercussions the case study discussed in this essay (the Romanian referendum in August 2012). However, if we were to confront our critical analysis of the culturalist ideological deployment with the unfolding of crisis in Ukraine, the argument for the relevance and the extreme material efficiency of the culturalist ideological frame seems rather confirmed by the tragic events. For what else should one read in the spectacular developments in Ukraine, if not, on the one hand, the spontaneous, yet interested on both parties, culturalist reading of a geopolitical and economic issue (the choice between EU and Russia as Ukraine's main exchange partner framed as a cultural civilizational clash between the land of the free and the empire of authoritarianism), and, on the other hand, the extreme, immense efficiency of this cultural mystification — its degeneration into a virtually enduring civil war — civil also in the sense that the stasis of the nation is lived and performed as an internal civilizational split. As for the question of whether this new "Cold War", as it is called, brought the Eastern European region back into the spotlight of historical and geopolitical relevance, this is debatable: true, Eastern Europe is no longer merely the internal periphery of Western capitalism, it is, or at least seems highly likely to become, the contested area between two assertive capitalist empires. It might be more relevant on a global stage; it's not necessarily more honourable.
2. In other words, there is nothing inherently specific to the Eastern European region in this culturalist treatment; as it will be shown later, this reading is rather mobile and can be extended or applied also to other (semi)peripheries — such as Southern Europe.
3. As Fleming (2000) rightly pointed out, "Hermann Keyserling's wry observation, 'If the Balkans did not exist, it would be necessary to invent them', was perhaps understated. Even though the Balkans do exist, they must be invented anyway. Simultaneously and tautologically, then, the Balkans are both fully known and wholly unknowable".
4. See the already consistent bibliography produced by this anthropological turn: Dunn (2004); Humphrey (2002); Mandel and Humphrey (2002).
5. Unfortunately, this culturalist explanation of continental economic divisions creates a situation where even the resistance to the EU's economic policies is couched in cultural terms, even in the works of some of the best contemporary critical theorists — see Agamben's (2014) recommendation that the solution lies in replacing the hegemonic German culture with the Latin one ("The Latin Empire Should Strike Back", http://www.presseurop.eu/en/content/article/3593961-latin-empire-should-strike-back).
6. As Lapavitsas pertinently deconstructed this cultural construction, the reason for Germany's surpluses and higher competitiveness is not the moral superiority of the German workers, their dedication and workaholism, but the pressure and squeezing of their wages (Lapavitsas et al.

2012). Hence, the cultural opposition between Germany and Greece conceals in fact a particular dynamic of class struggle — more on this in the closing paragraphs of the article.

7. The moralizing intentions and culturalist bias of the official political economy of the EU obviously lead to contradictory policies. See, for example, the EU's recommendation to Greece that it should increase the legal limit for working hours: this move, which effectively increases the unemployment rate, thus amplifying one of the problems it was supposed to solve, is nevertheless legitimized on the basis of its culturalist underlying idea, according to which the problem with the Greeks is that they are too lazy and do not work enough. For an extremely relevant discussion of the moralizing trend in the contemporary discourse of economics, see Fourcade et al. (2013), especially Wolfgang Streeck's piece.

8. Again, the cultural mystification of the class division did not come out of a clear blue sky. The primal scene of the Romanian nascent democracy was the infamous street battles in June 1990, opposing the anti-communist intellectuals, who were protesting against the staying in power of the old communist nomenklatura and its reluctance to modernize and Europeanize the state, and the miners, who intervened in order to defend the elected government, but also the rights and workplaces they enjoyed under socialism. Thus, the social conflict has been couched in cultural terms from the very beginning, as a conflict between the European and democratic culture of the enlightened middle class, and the corrupted culture of passivity and collectivism of the working class. The intellectuals took a beating in 1990. But everything since then, and especially the austerity measures implemented lately, have been seen by them as a well-deserved vengeance over their uncivilized opponents, and as a necessary lesson on the virtues of liberal individualism and social Darwinism.

9. Not incidentally, a similar position and recommendation have been expressed by financial capital through the voice of Morgan Stanley, in relation to Southern Europe: the economic problems of the Southern countries are actually political problems, rooted in the excess of democracy and anti-fascism that, for historical reasons, has been inscribed in their Constitutions (http://www.constantinereport.com/jp-morgan-to-eurozone-periphery-get-rid-of-your-pinko-anti-fascist-constitutions/).

References

Agamben, Giorgio. 2014. "The Latin Empire Should Strike Back." http://www.presseurop.eu/en/content/article/3593961-latin-empire-should-strike-back.

Ban, Cornel. 2012. "Sovereign Debt, Austerity, and Regime Change: The Case of Nicolae Ceausescu's Romania." *East European Politics & Societies* 26 (4): 743–776.

Blyth, Mark. 2013. *Austerity. The History of a Dangerous Idea.* New York: Oxford University Press.

Buden, Boris. 2009. *Zone des Übergangs Vom Ende des Postkommunismus* [*Passage Zone. On the End of Communism*]. Frankfurt am Main: Suhrkamp.

Chari, Sharad, and Katherine Verdery. 2009. "Thinking between the Posts: Postcolonialism, Postsocialism, and Ethnography after the Cold War." *Comparative Studies in Society and History* 51 (1): 6–34.

Croitoru, Lucian. 2012. *Jaful vs. Dreptul de a nu minți* [The Robbery vs. the Right Not to Tell Lies]. Bucharest: Curtea Veche.

Dunn, Elizabeth C. 2004. *Privatizing Poland: Baby Food, Big Business, and the Remaking of Labor*. Ithaca, NY: Cornell University Press.

Eyal, Gil, Ivan Szelenyi, and Eleanor Townsley. 1998. *Making Capitalism without Capitalists. The New Ruling Elites in Eastern Europe*. London: Verso.

Fleming, K. E. 2000. "Orientalism, the Balkans, and Balkan Historiography." *The American Historical Review* 105 (4): 1218–1233.

Fourcade, Marion, Philippe Steiner, Wolfgang Streeck, and Cornelia Woll. 2013. "Moral Categories in the Financial Crisis." *Socio-Economic Review* 11: 601–627.

Frank, Andre Gunder. 1992. "Nothing New in the East: No New World Order." *Social Justice* 19 (1): 34–61.

Humphrey, Caroline. 2002. *The Unmaking of Soviet Life: Everyday Economies after Socialism*. Ithaca, NY: Cornell University Press.

Lapavitsas, Costas, A. Kaltenbrunner, G. Lambrinidis, D. Lindo, J. Meadway, J. Michell, and J. P. Painceira. 2012. *Crisis in the Eurozone*. London: Verso.

Mandel, Ruth Ellen, and Caroline Humphrey. 2002. *Markets and Moralities: Ethnographies of Postsocialism*. Oxford: Berg.

Rogozanu, Costi. 2014. "Anticorruption, Another Name for Economic Abuse." *LeftEast*. http://www.criticatac.ro/lefteast/anti-corruption-another-name-for-economic-abuse/.

Tamás, G. M. 2014. "Dragi burghezi progresiști, dacă mai existați, nu vă temeți. Interviu [Dear Bourgeois Progressives, If You Still Exist, Do Not Be Afraid. Interview]." *CriticAtac*. http://www.criticatac.ro/25794/dragi-burghezi-progresiti-dac-mai-exis tai-nu-temei-interviu-cu-gm-tamas/.

Zizek, Slavoj. 2001. *Did Somebody Say Totalitarianism?* London: Verso.

Russian and East European Studies with a Finnish Flavour

Katalin Miklóssy

The end of the Cold War had a tremendous impact on the redefining of Russian and East European studies. The recalibration of national interest had an impact on the new prioritizations of research focus and agendas. This article shall discuss this phenomenon in Finland that has been traditionally a stronghold of the Russian and East European studies. The article analyses how Russian and East European Studies went through major transitions on three main levels (a) the politics of science; (b) the institutional structures in the university environment; and (c) the substance of scholarship.

Some disciplines are more embedded in the temporary context than others because they are more prone to changes in the political environment. Area studies can be described as a group of social sciences and humanities put together with a single meta-purpose: to grasp a geographical entity that is ultimately defined by political interest. Area studies have their roots in the colonial paradigm and hence display a straightforward connection to pragmatic political goals. To take full advantage of the resources of a distant territory and be able to apply suitable methods to govern, one had to combine a holistic knowledge of its geography, ethnography, politico-economic systems and culture. Hence, not only multidisciplinarity came along automatically, but also interdisciplinary discourse because the aim was to provide complex solutions for upcoming problems derived from the practice of control.

Nation states that lacked colonies did not have a use for area studies and the main interest of research was focused around the national agenda. Modern disciplines (humanities, social sciences, economics, legal studies) were

THE POLITICS OF EAST EUROPEAN AREA STUDIES

created, as we know them today, in the late eighteenth century in order to provide a backup for the national identity-building project, hence they were naturally nationally anchored (Hanak 1988). Such countries became interested in area studies relatively recently due to the fact that although they might be short of the colonial past, but most of them nevertheless have had an imperial experience as subjects. The need for an area approach might be seen also as showing caution regarding potential imperial threats and/or advantages. In particular, the Cold War hazard of superpowers for smaller countries had a significant impact on the awakening interest in the area gaze. To understand an intimidating great power in close vicinity as comprehensively as possible could be perceived as vital — hence this period was the heyday of area studies with an emphasis on prediction.

The end of the Cold War had a tremendous impact not only on the perception of the international context, but also on the redefining of the self and its relation to the area previously studied. Probably the most apt location for such changes had been Russian and East European studies, for obvious reasons. The old, problem-solving prescriptive nature of area studies re-entered in the early 1990s with the overall trend of economization of politics where threats and advantages were now understood in the context of national economic security and of business-led colonisation plans. Big firms from small countries could now acquire significant market shares abroad, bringing notable contributions to national economies. In order to operate efficiently, area studies were revisited from the points of view of advantages for the national interest. Due to the deteriorating economic situation in Europe after 2008, the prioritisation of what research is nationally important to focus on became even more accentuated. Economic crisis and political impatience with short-sighted and narrowly defined questions apparently have pointed towards the emergence of inner hierarchy amongst disciplines in area studies. The urge to create fast and circumscribed knowledge for political usage without a wider understanding of the sociocultural context have many resemblances in fact with Cold War area studies, and particularly with Sovietology. So, it seems that area studies have swung between predictive task during global crises and prescriptive duties in times of "normal" economic expansion.

The definition of *Eastern Europe* is also a constantly changing phenomenon that can be approached through the perceptions of the scientists working in area studies. How the body of experts describes the boundaries and content of the spatial entity reflects not only the current self-understanding of the discipline, but more importantly, reveals the considerations of the funding agencies behind scholarly communities. Since in most cases of European, and especially Nordic, academia science is conducted in universities or research institutes maintained by public spending, how political decision-makers see an area and its value for national interest has a direct impact on research. Although there is an obvious discursive relation between knowledge producers and knowledge users, nevertheless, what area is seen as vital to study "holistically" is always a sign of the political atmosphere and attitude. Furthermore, another side of the picture is that area researchers take advantage of the political interest and make a career out of it.

This article shall discuss this changing phenomenon in Finland which has traditionally been a stronghold of Russian and East European studies. Over the last decade, the Finns have become not only relatively (i.e. in relation to a population of 5.4 million), but also, in absolute terms, one of the major international players in Russian studies. The number of scholars, totalling about 5% of all Russian scientists in the world, is comparable with the quantity of UK and German scholars (Mustajoki 2013, 14). This figure indicates the massive investment the Finnish state carried out since the mid-1990s aimed at the understanding of the region. There is also an openly acknowledged symbiotic relationship between academic knowledge production, its applicability to society's practical needs and political will that may reward useful science with institutional security. The strength of this link can be explained partly by geopolitical position, with a 1313 km-long Russian border and a centuries-long common history, in addition to the fast growing Russian minority and intensive bilateral interaction in multiple fields.

The article analyses how Russian and East European Studies went through major transitions on three main levels: (a) the politics of science; (b) the institutional structures in the university environment; and (c) the substance of scholarship. These transformations took place in three waves: in the early 1990s, as a consequence of the collapse of the Soviet market; in the mid-1990s, due to Finnish EU-membership; and after the 2008 European financial crisis. As a narrative solution, we shall discuss the development of the political context that set the stage for institutional modifications and finally we shall turn towards the academic debates which reflected both political and institutional changes. These interwoven alterations can be best understood however if we recall first their Cold War background as a starting point.

Cold War shadows on Finnish scholarship

Finland looks back to a long history with Russia not only as a neighbouring country, but also as a Grand Duchy part of the Russian Empire (1809–1917) with an intertwined Russian speaking administrative and educated elite. This period established the tradition of a special, relation-based knowledge that was deepened with the help of generations of Russian emigrants. After the freshly gained independence in 1918, however, hate and suspicion against the previous overlords induced a general aim to distance the country mentally from Soviet-Russia and focus on nation-building. The academic circles were fully involved in the national endeavour and wanted to dispel the Russian heritage from university education also symbolically so that for instance the country's biggest university, the Imperial Alexander University, founded by the Tsar Alexander I, became the University of Helsinki in 1919. In this atmosphere, all Russian studies ended. The Soviet aggression against Finland in

1939 and later the surrendered Finnish territories, with the huge war compensations the country had to pay, spread a downright Russo-phobia that was not easy to overcome after Second World War.

Neutral Finland was a "friendly" state from the USSR's point of view; it had a Friendship, Co-operation and Mutual Assistance Treaty with the Soviet Union and belonged to the customs union of the Eastern Bloc. In 1947, when there was still a considerable danger that Finland would be drawn to the Soviet sphere of influence and become a satellite, President J.K. Paasikivi founded the *Soviet Institute* with the aim to restart scholarly investigation of the country's threatening neighbour. The Institute played an important role in reawakening academic interest because its main purpose was to establish and institutionalise bilateral cultural and scientific relations. However, these relations were sheltered from "unorthodox" or "hostile" interpretations of the USSR, hence publishing was effectively overlooked by the Finnish communists, the Soviet-Finnish Society and the Soviet Embassy, which exercised direct pressure on Finnish politics. Thus, research activities withered away and from the 1960s, the Institute confined itself to nurturing cultural relations (Melanko 1997; Perna 2002). Criticism of the Soviet regime was discouraged particularly during President Urho Kekkonen's period of office (1956—1981) and studies of power, security policy and Soviet history were unwanted disciplines. The Kekkonen era prioritised undisturbed working relations with the Soviet Union in order to safeguard Finnish trade interests (Niinimaa-Keppo 1997; Susiluoto 1997). One plausible example of this *Realpolitik* was the lack of political interest in establishing research institutes or university-level study programmes that would generate independent research, and consequently in such a politicised academic atmosphere, there was not much genuine intellectual interest in studying the Soviet Union either (Kivinen and Sutela 2000). Furthermore, in the 1960s and 1970s, parallel with the Western trend of leftist movements, there prevailed an aggressive domestic pro-Soviet atmosphere in Finnish universities that tried to discredit all "ill-fitting" scholarly works (Haavio-Mannila 1997; Luukkanen 2009; Tiusanen 2011). However, a rather well-functioning substitute was the Finnish-Soviet Committee for Scientific and Technological Co-operation with its several discipline-based working groups that provided an institutional framework enabling Finnish scholars to establish contacts to Russian colleagues on a grass-roots level without constant ideological control from above (Autio-Sarasmo 2013).

Over the years, the Finns gradually developed a solid expertise on the Soviet Union. While the term *Finlandisation* (Finnlandisierung), labelled by the German politician Franz-Josef Strauss,[1] put the country in a dubious light, nevertheless the Finns were able to take advantage of their special connections. Businessmen and government officials travelled across the USSR building up a solid stock of knowledge as a result of their practical dealings with the Russians. Not only was this kind of genuine "field know-how" unique in the West, but also the extended Finnish networks that penetrated deep into Russia's political and economic elites. This type of comprehension, however, had its shortcomings. On the one hand, since the information it produced was based on personal relations, it was not applicable for drawing a more general understanding of the wider context. In addition, the main sources of information were in many cases not academics but politicians, administrators and businessmen who had a good command of the Russian language and knew their own immediate field but were not theoretically oriented (Vihavainen 1991).

In this discouraging academic environment, the Finnish contribution to international theoretical discussions on Russia, particularly to Sovietology, was rather modest, but due to well-founded grass-roots connections, the Finns could gain incomparable collections of empirical data. The Western type of Sovietology was greatly deprecated as hostile propaganda regarding the Soviet Union, although there was an attempt to bring closer Finnish scholarship to the Western standards with a series of publications, named *Sovietological Studies*, assigned to the Institute of Foreign Policy in 1964. Due to Soviet pressure, the series was ended in 1977 and thereafter only a few individual scholars continued the Western paradigm. Regardless of the difficulties, there occurred top scholarship acquiring international recognition, such as the works of the economist Pekka Sutela, or the political scientists Ilmari Susiluoto and Jyrki Iivonen, the legal theorist Juha Tolonen, historians Heikki Kirkinen and Osmo Jussila, the linguist Arto Mustajoki, and cultural scientists Natalia Baschmakoff and Pekka Pesonen.

Sovietology was also not popular because the Finnish researchers worked within their disciplinary boundaries, maintained disciplinary networks and thus lacked the need for an all-embracing understanding. There were no scholarly arenas (journals, conferences or scientific societies) to support the area-gaze either. The Finnish Association for Russian and East European Studies was founded in 1989 as a sign of the increasing scholarly need to establish closer national networks in order to advance an area-approach and exchange ideas, now free of political interference. The Association provided a community for over 300 members and also a publishing arena, the Finnish Review of East European Studies (Idäntutkimus). For institutionalisation of the interdisciplinary endeavour, however, there was still a long way to go.

Reconsideration of the politics of science: between the New Russia and the EU

The Finnish politics of science regarding Russia basically served two goals. On the one hand, it had to provide useful information for the expansion of Finnish business and to ease the practice of bilateral relations with the unpredictable neighbouring great power. On the other hand, know-how was to assist the rise of Finnish international visibility and political significance in the European Union (EU).

Due to the collapse of the Soviet Union, Finland experienced a dramatic economic crisis because of the sudden loss of its Soviet markets. The general lesson regarding Russian studies was that the traditionally produced knowledge did not serve the needs of fast-changing realities and thus there emerged a subsequent urge to revisit the course of the politics of science. The new goal was to understand comprehensively the painful transition of Russia that had exhibited such a direct impact on Finnish economic performance. The Finnish Government decided in 1993 to direct considerable financial support in order to create a basis for updated knowledge and channelled 3.4 million euros for research through the Finnish Academy. This happened while the Finns were aware of the fact that at the same time Western academic interest in Russia and consequently institutional resources were decreasing. The first consistent programme supported 26 projects between 1995 and 2000, aiming to fulfil the needs of enterprises and the state administration with useful political and economic knowledge (Kangaspuro 2000; Evaluation of the Research Programme 2001; Oksanen, Lehvo, and Nuutinen 2003).

Meanwhile, Finland joined the EU in 1995 and this recalibrated Finnish political interest and therefore also the politics of science. The Finnish politicians were dedicated to raising the international profile of their country and one of the means was to direct EU attention to the geopolitical gateway position of Finland — at that time the only EU-country bordering Russia. Furthermore, there was a common assumption in European political circles that the Finns had special knowledge of Russia due to their historical relations (Vesikansa 1997). In particular, the wide networks of information concerning the Russian market were claimed to be outstanding in the EU (Kuparinen 1996). Since the EU displayed a long-standing interest in developing good neighbourhood relations with Russia, the Finns wished to become the bridge in between and make the most of the situation (Kivikari 1995; Austin 1996). This was a continuation of Finland's role between East and West during the Cold War, starting with the Helsinki process and the Conference of Security and Co-operation in Europe, where both sides trusted and needed the Finns' mediating services, thus elevating the small country's international status. Aligned with this conception and targeting also a new Nordic role, while the traditional Nordic cooperation was declining due to prioritising EU interests, the Finns launched the Northern Dimension initiative in 1997 that gained wider European support (Arter 2000, Heikkilä 2006). The initiative sought to increase cross-national co-operation in the Baltic and Barents Sea regions and one of its central aims was to bind Russia more effectively to the EU by partnership.

All these political aims had to be backed up with credible results, but the problem was that the level of Finnish scholarship was highly insufficient, since it had so far served national ends and thus was inappropriate for generating political capital on an international scale. The acknowledgement of this brought about a wide and steady consensus of the political elite at the time of PM Paavo Lipponen's so-called "rainbow administration" containing five parties from left to right which was in office for eight years (1995–2003). Consequently, the Minister of Education, Olli-Pekka Heinonen, launched an initiative to reform the institutional foundations of Russian studies entirely. This

THE POLITICS OF EAST EUROPEAN AREA STUDIES

included the strengthening of the position of the Russian language in all levels of the Finnish education system (HE 157/1996), increasing exchange programmes and bilateral cooperation. In addition, a central research agency, the Aleksanteri Institute[2] was established in 1996 assigned with an undertaking to create new scholarship based on interdisciplinary investigation in order to acquire a more profound and sustainable knowledge base. It was to reorganise systematically the training of future experts at the masters and doctoral levels. In addition, the Institute was also endowed with a mission to take into consideration practical interests in the design of academic research and thus to serve economic actors, the state administration and the civil sphere. This meant that social sciences received special attention at the cost of humanities. To ensure societal sensitivity and to channel the immediate needs of society, politicians and economic figures were invited to the advisory board, (including ministers, industrialists and even George Soros), a feature that was rather unconventional at that time in the Nordic university context (Kivinen 1996; Ruoppila 1996). Interestingly, at a time when great Russian research centres in the West were diminishing due to the recalibrations of funding, the Finns started to invest massively in Russian studies.

This, however, was not welcomed unanimously by the academic community because a considerable resistance towards area research appeared. Passionate polemics burst out about the proper ways of achieving Russia-expertise and the new Institute was criticised of being oriented too much to social sciences and forgetting about history and culture which were argued to be indispensable while dealing with Russians. From the traditional disciplinary perspectives area, studies were highly dubious and embodied an immanently arrogant scientific approach. The historian Timo Vihavainen pointed out the questionable value of any scholarly endeavour whose purpose is to construct one-dimensional, simplified "truths" about another country's history, politics or society in order to produce *useful* information for practical applications. Science is nothing but continuous discourse between different interpretations over a complex reality. If there existed an imaginary *Finnish studies*, it would be highly unlikely if any such expert could be found in Finland, Vihavainen (1997) stated. The sociologist Timo Piirainen drew attention to the questionable ethics of Russian studies that characteristically focus on problems and peculiarities, and raise oddities or differences in comparison to a supposed Western normalcy. Moreover, there is still an essentially colonialist feature in the scientific conduct where researchers are travelling across a vast country, gathering data and gaining information without the faintest idea how they are going to use it (Piirainen 1997).

The research infrastructure was strengthened also by non-university institutions. The research section of the Bank of Finland, the Institute for Economies in Transition and the Finnish Institute of International Affairs are both maintained by the public budget with their main purpose being to ensure fast and applicable information for economic and political actors in contrast to the characteristically slower knowledge production of the universities.

Fine-tuning of research funding principles was carried out as well. The evaluation report of the above-mentioned research programme (1995–2000) of the Finnish Academy pointed out the division between need-driven Russian research and curiosity-led East European projects, which also reflected a change in emphasis. From the 26 projects, only 2 were directed to studying Eastern Europe and 3 to conduct Russian–Eastern European comparison, the other 21 projects investigated Russia from different angles (Kangaspuro 2000). The report reminded that Eastern Europe served *"as a component or compara-tor in large multi-regional and multi-disciplinary projects"* (Evaluation of Research Programme 2001) and predicted the gradual marginalisation of the area in the politics of science.

In the early 2000s, the EU accession of the ex-Eastern Bloc countries and the international debate on the "core and periphery" type of structural changes in the EU raised the threat that the Finnish position would turn periph-eral in the more numerous European community. This situation had relevance also for the Finnish political capital of Russian studies since the new EU mem-bers had wider experience and thorough field knowledge of Russia. The Finns obviously could not anticipate that the ex-communist states in their Western enthusiasm had consciously destroyed the institutional basis of their Russian studies. Since seemingly, the Finnish competitive advantage was fading away, more adequate research was needed. As a new asset, a Cross-Border University was established in 2004 near to the Russian border, in Joensuu, providing a double Masters programme in co-operation with five Finnish and two Russian universities, aiming to create cross-expertise that could further practical interaction (Mustajoki 2007).

In addition, in 2003, the Finnish Academy started a new multidisciplinary Russian programme "Changing Russia" – now exclusively focused on Russia – and allocated 8 million euros helping indirectly the Finnish EU objectives regarding the Northern Dimension initiative (Ohjelmamuistio 2003). The nov-elty of the programme was that now natural and life sciences were supported after the previous emphasis on humanities and social sciences. The fund ran until 2007 – until after the Finnish EU presidency, which stressed Russian issues and introduced a new phase of the Northern Dimension project aiming to improve Russian commitment to it (Heikkilä 2006; Mustajoki 2007). Conduct-ing such a central mediating role had relevance also for reflecting on European agendas more sensitively. Hence, in addition to the Finnish priority interest in business relations, energy policy, justice and human rights topics started to enter the academic focus in the late 2000s.

After the 2008 financial crisis, the Finnish interest has turned even more energetically towards the East. Expanding trade relations and business in Russia were to provide a safety belt for the Finnish economy, not to mention of the fast-growing Russian investments in Finland. Along with global trends, the general economisation of politics is reflected in the policy of science by favouring more specialisation and bilateral research co-operations based on joint funding opportunities (see, for example, Yhteishankehaku 2013).

Lately, there emerged a new aspect which emphasises the need for more diversified knowledge of Russia. According to Markku Kivinen, there are obviously different purposes of expertise in the various fields of trade, the public sector, tourism and civil encounters that require reactions from educators on different levels with a more flexible and colourful schooling system than the contemporary simplified emphasis on plain university/college education (Kivinen 2013). Russia-expertise was to become a nation-wide experience that would display a completely new quality of know-how and stronger competitive advantage for Finland.

New institutionalisation of research-based education

There is a unique Finnish way to operationalize the political goals at the level of education. It can be argued that the Finnish model is extremely successful because it is cost-effective, consistent and innovative. The institutional infrastructure was designed to decrease academic competition between universities and establish a win-win situation with a genuine striving for cooperation. In the mid-1990s, centralisation took place combining the sporadic knowledge, carried out by individual researchers scattered around the country at different universities, and identifying the obvious gaps regarding the needs of society. In 1998, the first Masters' Programme in Russian and Eastern European Studies and also Graduate School (later Doctoral Programme), attached to the Aleksanteri Institute, were established with the purpose of reorganising higher education. The endeavour was based on the co-operation of 12 universities with an underlined aim of making the curriculum more effective through the co-ordination of one centre (Kaakkuriniemi 1999).

The institutional changes induced by the fluctuation of the politics of science reflected a double goal, national and international, on the different levels of expert production. Masters' education was to serve, first and foremost, national purposes regarding trade, businesses and administration. The aim was to rethink what kind of expertise students would need in order to meet the requirements of the labour market regarding the fast-growing Finnish business interest in Russia. It became fairly obvious that "traditional" area studies represented by such model-provider British centres as the University College London School of Slavonic and East European Studies (UCL SSEES) or the Birmingham Centre of Russian and East European Studies offering a general degree of *Russian and East European studies* were not what the Finns aspired towards. The Finnish labour market did not appreciate generalists; therefore, the main objective of the new Finnish School was to combine strong disciplinary training with an extended understanding of the regional context. The school enriched the major subject with an additional area specific knowledge in the form of a minor subject. Hence, the new masters graduated from their own disciplines as economists, lawyers, journalists, political scientists, sociologists and historians while the school strengthened their language skills and provided an extra knowledge of the area. Thus, economists and lawyers had solid knowledge of Russian economics or the legal system, political scientists of Russian politics, etc. In addition, all had training covering the main lines of history, culture, society and the politico-economic system in order to understand the wider societal context as well. Obviously, the other side of the coin was the *safety-belt characteristic* of the system whereby the new masters graduates could always rely on their disciplinary background if the Russia-related labour market could not employ them.

This model worked extremely well, actually exceeding expectations. Between 1998 and 2012, 285 students graduated from the Master's school and according to the co-ordinator Hanna Peltonen's estimation, *"nearly 90% of the graduates found employment almost immediately and over 60% are working in occupational fields that concentrate on the area"* (Peltonen 2013[3] Statistics of the Finnish Masters' Programme). The intensity of the two-year master's education with summer and winter schools, joint courses and study trips establishes strong group identification and lasting networks (Peltonen 2013). Thus, over the years, the school created a new generation of experts employed in the area, trained to apply an interdisciplinary approach and to maintain close links to their peers across the field. This condition can be claimed as a rising competitive edge for Finnish economic actors, particularly, but it provides also a more complex understanding for political decision-makers and administrative personnel enabling them to deal with this region properly.

The Aleksanteri Institute was also a response to the mounting situation where doctoral students had to get education from abroad, especially from UCL SSEES (Ruoppila 1996). The new doctoral programme was to provide the theoretical basis for a more elaborated Finnish expertise regarding Russia particularly played out on the international arena. The high efficiency rate of the doctoral education was rather convincing: between 1998 and 2012, the school produced 45 PhDs in a great variety of disciplinary fields (Statistics of the Doctoral Programme 2013). Due to the peculiar rigidity of the Finnish labour market, however, whereas freshly graduated masters find jobs easily, PhDs have considerable difficulties in getting stable positions. Employers refrain from hiring "over-qualified" experts without practical experience who have relied mostly on theoretical training. Correspondingly, universities are not capable to absorb the increasing number of new scholars either. By investing into an internationally acknowledged, high-standard education with language skills and double-edged qualification (i.e. in their disciplines and the area), area experts are competitive on the international markets (Jänis-Isokangas 2013).

The latest development in Russian studies is interlinked with the overall market-driven Finnish university reform started in 2010 (Yliopistolaki 558/2009). Since the new legislation forced the universities to rationalise budgetary considerations and search for donors from the private sector, it affected the institutional structure of Russian and East European studies as well. The universities — who are not immune to their benefactors' preferences — had to make tough decisions about what type of education they can afford, hence

THE POLITICS OF EAST EUROPEAN AREA STUDIES

there emerged a specialisation in area studies (Lappalainen 2012). So, for instance, the University of Eastern Finland took on border research, University of Tampere is concentrating on cultural studies and international relations, Lappeenranta University of Technology is focusing besides technology on business studies, University of Lapland on legal studies, etc. This, on the other hand, reflects also the new phase and conceptual transformation of Russian studies marking a departure from a wider multidisciplinary platform and a prioritisation of disciplines evaluated according to their "value-for-money".

Scholarly discourses on the contemporary value of area studies

Probably the most passionate debates over the quality of scholarship over the last decade dealt with three main agendas: (a) from what perspective research is conducted; (b) what is worth exploring; and (c) how it should be studied. All of these topics uncovered indirectly the core challenge, the overtly political nature of area studies.

(a) *What is the "Right" Approach?*

The political undertone of Russian studies has been a particularly sensitive issue due to the earlier mentioned Cold War *Finnlandisierung* which still casts long shadows on the evaluation of research. In 1996, a new book (transl. "Russia. Giant Drifting") was published by a political scientist and two foreign correspondents focusing on the problems of Russian development (Sailas, Susiluoto, and Valkonen 1996). Heated debates about the "right" angle or "justified" approach revealed that coming to terms with the past is an unfinished business in Finnish society. This became visible in the scholarly "post-Finlandisation" arm wrestling. Interestingly, the criticism of "post-Finlandisation" meant first a converse Finlandisation, where it was claimed that *ex-communists* sympathised with the old Soviet regime and had therefore turned against the transition process of the New Russia picturing everything in an overtly critical tone. This judgement, raised by younger generation of sociologists Bäckman (1996) and Rotkirch (1996), aimed to undermine the expertise of the authors with politicised arguments. The charges were answered by historians Häikiö (1996) and Vihavainen (1997), who argued that any contemporary issue cannot be studied without considering the burdens of the Soviet past. Thus, disregarding the wider temporal comparative angle from the analysis and investigations would create only shallow sociological snapshots. The polemics over the book coincided with the launching of the Aleksanteri Institute which many questioned not only because of its social science focus, but also because the director of the Institute, the sociologist Markku Kivinen looked back to a left-wing youth.

Later during the 2010s, in the follow-up debate, the accusations actually turned upside down and were directed towards the "leftists" because of their "too mild" criticism of Russia in the Putin era, which reminded some scholars of the arrogant pro-Soviet intellectual movement during the Kekkonen era (Luukkanen 2010b, 2013). This conflict however grew out of proportion and was targeted towards the younger generation of researchers who were in fact born in the 1980s but were working under the guidance of mentors with an allegedly leftist past (Luukkanen 2010a).

This controversy has been colouring the approach to Russian society and its political establishment. Besides the possibility that categorical criticism might actually reproduce black-and-white images and the narrow understanding typical of the mentality of the Cold War, it also standardises the Western-looking glass where Russian development is incomprehensible. In contrast, approaches where Russia is seen from within and not from the point of view of Western moral superiority are denounced as being "leftist" and hence as not credible scientifically. This kind of stigmatisation might prevent a more complex understanding of Russian processes.

(b) *Revisiting areas*

There is an immanent problem in all area studies: How one defines a space reflects more of one's understanding of the World than of the region itself. Thus, reconceptualization of areas reveals an intellectual change and its temporal context, but it has also a consequence for the identity of area studies *per se*. There is a new transformation in the scholarly interest revisiting the area worth studying.

Although, the position of Russia has never been questioned in Finland, nevertheless, there is a linkage to the ongoing global debates on how the East should be perceived and there are new reflections on the spatial connections of Russia, pushing the focus of research further to the East. The "travelling concept" *Eurasia* has introduced lately a broader interrelation lowering mental boundaries. China is still studied separately from Russia, but there are new attempts to find overlapping issues like comparative approaches between Chinese and Russian current development patterns, such as. "At the Crossroads of Post-Communist Modernisation" (Pursiainen 2012). In addition to the East, there is also the North as a new angle to investigate interconnectedness. The Arctic increasingly gains attention which continues the same tracks of the Northern Dimension Initiative.

When we invent new terms, however, it might come with a price. Grouping for instance relatively wide geographical entities such as "Eurasia" has relevance not only for the meaning of distinction, but also for the fact that it is the method that might become the core identifier of area studies in the end. *Eurasia* displays a fluidity of demarcation, which in an umbrella sort of way gives elbowroom for various, even fast-changing sub-conceptualisations. Moreover, defining a vast region under the same title obscures the usefulness of substance, hence the ultimate connotation relies on the method of multidisciplinary inquiry.

THE POLITICS OF EAST EUROPEAN AREA STUDIES

The most radical change took place in relation to the concept of Eastern Europe. Interestingly, in the Nordic context, there have been differences regarding what regions should be included under the term. Hence, for example, University of Södertörn (Sweden) is calling its institution the Centre of Baltic and East European Studies, whereas the Aleksanteri Institute is the Finnish Centre for Russian and East European studies. The message embedded is that according to the Finnish understanding, Russia is not Eastern Europe, whereas for the Swedes, the Baltic does not belong to Eastern Europe while Russia obviously does. The most significant question in this regard has been how the "new EU-countries" that used to belong to the East during the Cold War should now be categorised (Comisso and Gutierrez 2004). This trend is also in line with current international discourses (Applebaum 2013; The End of the Story? 2013) that question the dubious aspects of using the label "East" on countries that have aligned with Transatlantic and EU institutions and where naming relates conceptually to the "post-communist" or "transition" phenomena. Hence, there are strong arguments that actually this region should be dealt within the realm of European Studies.

The Finnish institutional structures have evaded taking sides in this debate, but this can be seen also as a strategy to save the study of East Central Europe, the Baltic States and the Balkans, established (see the "ECEBB-programme") according to an agenda placing them as a differentiated entity from the all-embracing European studies. It reflects nevertheless the perception that this region has still something in common in contrast to the Western half of the EU, although the post-communist transitional past is less recalled if at all. This view actually provides a new platform to revisit regional development patterns in different contemporary horizontal contexts. Eastern Europe, on the other hand, relates also to the belt between the new EU countries and Russia containing Ukraine, Belorussia and Moldova. It remains to be seen if we witness the label "Eastern Europe" fading away or actually gaining power due to the increasing democracy problems in the ECEBB area.

In the Finnish academic context, there is strong emphasis on Russia in contrast to the Baltic Sea region that equally bears significance politically, economically and environmentally for Finland. During the past two decades, there were excellent individual scholars scattered around the country focusing on the Baltic states, such as the historians Seppo Zetterberg and Marko Lehti, the political scientists Marja Nissinen and Kristi Raik, sociologist Laura Asmuth, and the economist Urpo Kivikari. Partly to gather these forces, the Centre for Baltic Sea issues (Centrum Balticum) was founded in 2006 and was situated in Turku. It operates as an independent think tank and concentrates on practical questions and applied research. It generates discourse amongst scientists, economic actors, policy-makers and civil organisations. Due to the geographical vicinity of Baltic universities, it seems that, with the exception of a few specialists, the Finns settled on basic research and top-level expertise has been imported through collaborative arrangements. Nevertheless, it has been widely acknowledged that Finnish enterprises and authorities have needs for Baltic experts, hence a multidisciplinary MA programme was established in 2011 at the University of Helsinki combining the area of East Central Europe, the Balkans and the Baltic States. The Baltic states have started to reidentify themselves in new spatial contexts, partly with the Nordic cultural hemisphere and partly with East Central Europe, and academic connections have been consistently strengthened. This conscious attachment might bear relevance to the future scope of area studies, such as for Nordic studies, for instance.

Regarding Russian and East European studies, there appear fresh initiatives but also old problems in new cloths. Teuvo Teivainen has suggested that — aligned with current international developments in Latin American area, studies which is transforming into *Latin American and Latino* Studies — perhaps Russian studies could include into its scope also the Russian population living in Finland (Teivainen 2013). This view would undoubtedly strengthen the contemporary emphasis on interactions and the transregional gaze. Similarly, there is a new euphemism that has the potential to revisit Eastern Europe conceptually: the *Europe Between*. The notion has been in use over a decade ago mostly by historians Saarikoski (1994, 1999) and El Ramly (1999) but it faded away as a reflection of the Eastern enlargement of the EU and the strengthening Western angle in the region. The idea that between Russian- and German-speaking lands, there is a belt where Eastern and Western characteristics mix and create a special region itself is older though (Szücs 1983). This concept however caries a special significance, namely that Finland is thought to belong to this area due to its historical experience under Swedish and Russian rule and not least its Cold War "Finlandisation" era. Still, in the latest encounters, also by the author of this article, the Europe Between notion has been applied either to the Eastern Bloc satellites or to the new EU countries with troubled democratisation (see Miklóssy 2010, 2011). This label was able to avoid the simplified picturing of the Eastern Bloc and also the much-debated "post-communist" reasoning.

(c) *Methods of conduct*

There occurs a new self-reflection in area studies indicating two main concerns that represent actually the core elements of identity of this field. On the one hand, it deliberates the overall scholarly relation to its object. On the other hand and equally importantly, it constitutes an active search for finding new paths methodologically.

Area studies genuinely display an asymmetrical relation in the endeavour of *"investigating the OTHER"*. The main question is how one understands otherness: Is it a dialogical or diametrical relationship? In a dialogical connection, the researcher's self and the research object are in continuous interaction and maintain a value-flexible relation. In a diametrical nexus, the self and the other represent opposite values, where the other can be seen as a threat for the self or what the self stands for.

Regarding Russian and East European studies, the diametrical attitude played a significant role since the mid-1990s influenced by the widely spread perception of the EU as a normative power. This phenomenon was particularly present during the transition period and appeared as "we know it all" arrogance. Paternalistic sentiment, however, blurred the scholarly sight and produced sometimes inadequate results carried away by a prescriptive stance. However, the so-called transition literature was never strongly absorbed by the Finnish scholars because the transition paradigm was seen as a substitute for *Sovietology* which never took off in Finland.

By the mid-2000s, the European normative-ness started to fade away (Diez 2005; Manners 2006) and with it the asymmetric attitude. Even though there are still strong views about the European mission especially in the study of democratisation and human rights supported by politicians and followed by academics, still there is a new opening up towards fresh, more balanced ways of investigating Russian and Eastern European development. In this approach, the angle does not exclusively and self-evidently rely anymore on Western comparisons, but the context is the area itself with respect to long-term development patterns and indigenous conceptions (see the site of a mega-project with over 40 researchers "Choices of Russian Modernisation").

In addition to the above-mentioned relation to the object of study, there is an ongoing discussion about methodology as well. There is a deeply rooted suspicion regarding the added value of area studies in comparison to disciplines. However, it has been acknowledged that interdisciplinary research is more likely to induce scientific breakthroughs and hence the Finnish university reform has lowered traditional disciplinary boundaries and piled them up into larger departments. In addition, the Academy of Finland also rewards multidisciplinary project proposals. Even though that "interdisciplinary discourse" is the key requirement of contemporary scholarship, nevertheless it is more difficult to put the *mantra* into practice in the traditionally discipline-based thinking of the Finnish academic environment.

Area studies, on the other hand, have always relied on crossing boundaries horizontally and vertically at the same time. Horizontally, area studies are immanently international with an underlying comparative gaze on the other and the self. Vertically, it represents a certain flexibility to various disciplines. From the traditional disciplines' point of view, however, area studies were only a bunch of disciplines without real benefit of interdisciplinary understanding. Part of this criticism is well grounded because area studies centres were established in the Nordic context only in the late 1990s and thus the first generation of researchers were trained in disciplinary thinking. Hence, interdisciplinary practice had to be invented in operation. Fortunately, the complexity of contemporary problems in fact assisted this process with the realisation that single disciplines are insufficient to provide useful answers. It seems that there emerges a new interdisciplinary thinking that is coming from a novel ability to relate to problem-solving transferring the angle from disciplinary anchored tools to the problem in question with openness to innovative solutions. On the other hand, one could argue that this is actually the renaissance of an old idea where area studies started in the late nineteenth century due to colonialist task-driven needs. Still, it can be claimed that we are reaching out towards a new methodology where complexity is reflected upon more carefully at the expense of holistic oversimplification. The reason for this change can be found partly in the fact that our current endeavour is influenced by a more balanced under-standing of *Otherness*, and the partly because our disciplines' boundaries are lowering and they are gradually altering into *interdisciplines*.

What is particularly Finnish in Russian and East European Studies?

This article started with the claim that there is a difference between ordinary interdisciplinary discourse and area studies because the latter is always embedded in a purpose of holistic understanding of a politically defined terri-tory often for political ends. The example of Finland demonstrated that the various national and international goals have had a rather straightforward con-nection to academic conduct through institutional modifications. The Finns traditionally have invested a great deal in education and in an information society which has guaranteed their international competitiveness and welfare. They have also understood that knowledge can turn a small country into a relatively big international player if the know-how is efficiently applied, consis-tently marketed and properly sold, and especially if it regards an area that seems incomprehensible from the Western point of view.

Finnish knowledge of Russia has been built on the long-standing bilateral col-laborations and wide networks that all gave a special flavour to the information produced. The acknowledgement that neighbourhood bears grave consequences for Finnish development resulted not only in intensive monitoring, but also the deeper understanding and realisation that studying Russia is in fact studying Finnish options. This is why for instance there is comparably more research on bilateral relations and a high-tuned sensitivity in following closely even minor changes in political structures. Thus, Finnish interest in area studies is not susceptible to international mood changes or even EU-policy alterations.

Disclosure statement

No potential conflict of interest was reported by the author.

Notes

1. The term referred to Soviet intentions to intervene in the internal affairs of the neighbouring small country. Franz-Josef Strauss's article on Finlandization was published widely on 23 February 1972 in *The Times* in a joint edition with *La Stampa, Die Welt, and Le Monde*.

THE POLITICS OF EAST EUROPEAN AREA STUDIES

2. The name referred to the old name of the University of Helsinki (Imperial Alexander University), which was the host institution of the Aleksanteri Institute.
3. Ms. Peltonen explained that this figure is based on a fairly well-grounded but not full-proven estimation since the follow-up records have been prepared only periodically.

References

Applebaum, Anne. 2013. "Does Eastern Europe Exist?" *Prospect*, March 20.
Arter, David. 2000. "Small State Influence Within the EU: The Case of Finland's 'Northern Dimension Initiative'." *JCMS: Journal of Common Market Studies* 38 (5): 667–697.
Austin, Daniel F. C. 1996. *Finland as a Gateway to Russia: Issues in European Security.* Aldershot: Avebury.
Autio-Sarasmo, Sari. 2013. "Knowledge through the Iron Curtain: Soviet Scientific-technical Cooperation with Finland and Germany." In *Reassessing Cold War Europe*, edited by Sari Autio-Sarasmo and Katalin Miklóssy, 66–82. London: Routledge.
Bäckman, Johan. 1996. "Venäjä jäkisuomettuneen näkökulman mukaan paha ja per-verssi maa" ["Russia is an Evil and Pervert Country According to Post-finlandised Point of View"]. *Helsingin Sanomat 4.5.1996.*
Choices of Russian Modernisation. Finnish Centre of Excellence in Russian Studies. 27 June 2013. http://www.helsinki.fi/aleksanteri/crm/research-plan.html.
Comisso, Ellen, and Brad Gutierrez. 2004. "Eastern Europe or Central Europe? Exploring a Distinct Regional Identity." In *The Politics of Knowledge. Area Studies and the Disciplines*, edited by David Szanton, 262–313. Berkeley: University of California Press.
Diez, Thomas. 2005. "Constructing the Self and Changing Others: Reconsidering 'Norma-tive Power Europe'." *Millennium - Journal of International Studies* 33 (3): 613–636.
ECEBB-program: East Central European, Balkan and Baltic Studies, University of Helsinki. 27 June 2013. http://www.helsinki.fi/aleksanteri/english/studies/ecebb/in dex.html.
El Ramly, Ranya. 1999. "Väli-Eurooppa, Jugoslavia ja Kroatia" ["Europe Between, Yugoslavia and Croatia"]. In *Syitä ja seurauksia. Jugoslavian hajoaminen ja seuraa-javaltioiden nykytilanne*, edited by Katalin Miklóssy, 99–108. Helsinki: Kikimora Publications.
'Evaluation of the Research Programme for Russia and Eastern Europe 1995–2000, Panel Report.' 2001. *Publication of the Academy of Finland 4/2001*, 15 March 2013. http://www.aka.fi/Tiedostot/Tiedostot/Julkaisut/Russia%20and%20Eastern%20Europe %20Evaluation.pdf.
Haavio-Mannila, Elina. 1997. "Suomalaiset ovat tutkineet itänaapuria" ["Finns had been Studying their Eastern Neighbor"]. *Helsingin Sanomat 5.2.1997.*
Häikiö, Martti. 1996. "'Jälkisuomettuminen' Öhmanin tapaus" ["Post-finlandisation: The Case of Öhman"]. *Kanava* 6: 327–328.
Hanak, Harry. 1988. "Preface." In *Historians and Nation-Builders. Central and South-East Europe*, edited by Dennis Deletant and Harry Hanak, vi–ix. London: MacMillan.
HE. 157/1996. *Hallituksen esitys Eduskunnalle laiksi vieraskielisistä yksityisistä kou-luista annetun lain 2§ muuttamisesta.* 24 June 2013. http://www.finlex.fi/fi/esityk set/he/1996/19960157.
Heikkilä, Markku. 2006. *The Northern Dimension*. Helsinki: Europe Information 188C, Ministry of Foreign Affairs of Finland.
Jänis-Isokangas, Ira. 2013. E-mail interview with the author. 6 June 2013.

THE POLITICS OF EAST EUROPEAN AREA STUDIES

Kaakkuriniemi, Tapani. 1999. "Nätverksbyggande kring östforskning" ["Building Networks Around East European Studies"]. *Nordisk Ostforum* 4: 69–73.

Kangaspuro, Markku. 2000. "Projects of the Programme of the Academy of Finland in 1995–2000." In *Russia: More Different than Most*, edited by Markku Kangaspuro, 287–328. Helsinki: Kikimora.

Kivikari, Urpo. 1995. From a Giant to a Gateway in East-West Trade: Finland's Adaptation to Radical Changes in Eastern Europe. Turku: Turun Kauppakorkeakoulu, Sarja C Keskustelua.

Kivinen, Markku. 1996. "Speech at the Opening Seminar of the Aleksanteri Institute." Archive of the Aleksanteri Institute, University of Helsinki, Finland, September 19.

Kivinen, Markku. 2013. "Minkälaisia asiantuntijoita Suomi tarvitsee?" ["What Kind of Experts does Finland Need"]. In *VIE osaaminen yhteiskuntaan*, edited by Iiris Virtasalo, et al., 58–61. Helsinki: Ovet.

Kivinen, Markku, and Pekka Sutela. 2000. "Introduction." In *Russia: More Different than Most*, edited by Markku Kangaspuro, 9–26. Helsinki: Kikimora.

Kuparinen, Alpo. 1996. "Speech at the Opening Seminar of the Aleksanteri Institute." Archive of the Aleksanteri Institute, University of Helsinki, Finland, September 19.

Lappalainen, Tuomo. 2012. "Kuinka yliopistouudistuksesta tuli kaikkien aikojen fiasco?" ["How did the Univeristy Reform Become a Complete Disaster?"] *Suomen Kuvalehti — Verkkojulkaisu 30.10.2012*. 6 June 2013. http://suomenkuvalehti.fi/jutut/koti maa/kuinka-yliopistouudistuksesta-tuli-kaikkien-aikojen-fiasko.

Luukkanen, Arto. 2009. *Muutosten Venäjä*. Helsinki: Edita.

Luukkanen, Arto. 2010a. "Vasemmistolainen Venäjä-tutkimus on matkalla historian roskalavalle" ["Leftist Russia-scholarship is on its Way to the Dust Bind of History"]. *Helsingin Sanomat. 8.6.2010.*

Luukkanen, Arto. 2010b. *Suomi Venäjän taskussa* [*Finland in the Pocket of Russia*]. Helsinki: WSOY.

Luukkanen, Arto. 2013. "Aatu ja Stalin — Suomen parhaat frendit" ["Adolf and Stalin: Best Friends of Finland"]. *Uusi Suomi. 17.5.2013. Puheenvuoro*. 29 May 2013. http://ar toluukkanen.puheenvuoro.uusisuomi.fi/140433-aatu-ja-stalin-suomen-parhaat-frendit.

Manners, Ian. 2006. "Normative Power Europe Reconsidered: Beyond the Crossroads." *Journal of European Public Policy* 13 (2): 182–199.

Melanko, Valdemar. 1997. "50th Anniversary of the Finnish Institute for Russian and East European Studies." *Idäntutkimus* 2: 72–73.

Miklóssy, Katalin. 2010. "Crossing Boundaries in the East during the Cold War." In *The East and the Idea of Europe*, edited by Katalin Miklóssy and Pekka Korhonen, 69–92. Newcastle upon Tyne: Cambridge Scholars Publishers.

Miklóssy, Katalin. 2011. "Demokratia jäi puolitiehen uusissa EU-maissa. EU-perheen kuopukset 1/6" ["Half-way Democratization in the New EU-Countries"]. *Helsingin Sanomat Vieraskynä* 28.6.2011.

Mustajoki, Arto. 2007. "Yliopistojen Venäjä-yhteistyön ja Venäjä-osaamisen kehittäminen" ["Developing Russian Expertise and Cooperation of the Universities"]. *Opetusministeriön työryhmämuistioita ja selvityksiä 2007:11.* 24 June 2013. http://www.minedu.fi/ex port/sites/default/OPM/Julkaisut/2007/liitteet/tr11.pdf?lang=fi.

Mustajoki, Arto. 2013. "Suomen Venäjä-osaaminen parempaan käyttöön" ["Taking Better use of Russian expertise in Finland"]. In *Vie osaaminen yhteiskuntaan: Venäjän ja itäisen Euroopan tuntemuksen uudet suuntaviivat*, edited by Iiris Virtasalo, et al., 12–19. Helsinki: Ovet.

Niinimaa-Keppo, Aila. 1997. "Sovietologian avain valokeilan ulkopuolelta" ["The Key of Sovietology can be found Outside of Spotlight"]. *Helsingin Sanomat 24.2.1997.*

THE POLITICS OF EAST EUROPEAN AREA STUDIES

'Ohjelmamuistio.' (Finnish Academy, Memo of the Russian Research programme). 2003. 15 March 2013. http://www.aka.fi/fi/A/Ohjelmat-ja-yhteistyo/Tutkimusohjelmat/Paattyneet/Venaja/Tutkimusohjelmamuistio/.

Oksanen, Timo, Annamaija Lehvo, and Anu Nuutinen. 2003. *Suomen Tieteen Tila ja Taso — Katsaus tutkimustoimintaan ja tutkimuksen vaikutuksiin 2000-luvun alussa, Suomen Akatemian julkaisuja 9/2003* [*The Situation and Level of Finnish Scholarship: Overview of the Finnish Research Activity and its Impact in the Beginning of 2000s*]. 20 May 2013. http://www.aka.fi/Tiedostot/Tiedostot/Julkaisut/9_03%20Suomen%20tieteen%20tila%20a%20taso.pdf.

Peltonen, Hanna. 2013. *Interview*. 29 April 2013.

Perna, Ville. 2002. *Tehtävänä Neuvostoliitto. Opetusministeriön Neuvostoinstituutin roolit suomalaisessa politiikassa 1944–1992* [*The Task is the Soviet Union: The Role of the Ministry of Education in the Soviet Institute in Finnish Politics 1944–1992*]. Helsinki: Venäjän ja Itä-Euroopan instituutti.

Piirainen, Timo. 1997. "Ymmärtäminen ja kriittisyys" ["Understanding and Criticism"]. *Idäntutkimus* 4: 3–5.

Pursiainen, Christer, ed. 2012. *At the Crossroads of Post-Communist Modernisation. Russia and China in Comparative Perspective*. New York: Palgrave Macmillan.

Rotkirch, Anna. 1996. "Jälkisuomettuminen vastaan venäläinen nationalismi" ["Post-finlandisation Against Russian Nationalism"]. *Ulkopolitiikka* 2: 22–23.

Ruoppila, Samppo. 1996. "Aleksanteri-instituutti. Tiedepanos parempaan Venäjän ja Itä-Euroopan tuntemukseen" ["Aleksanteri Institute: Investment in Science for Better Russian and East European Expertise"]. *Valtiotieteilijä* 4: 44–45.

Saarikoski, Vesa. 1994. "Väli-Eurooppa: geokulttuurinen ja historiallinen näkökulma Venäjän ja Saksan välisen Euroopan nykytilaan" ["Europe Between: Geocultural and Historical View to the Current Situation of the Area Between Russia and Germany"]. In *Euroopan murroksia*, edited by Jyrkki Kärönen, 97–140. Tampere: Rauhan ja konfliktin tutkimuslaitos.

Saarikoski, Vesa. 1999. *Väli-Eurooppa kylmän sodan jälkeen* [*Europe Between After the Cold War*]. *Suomen Akatemia: Seminaari 7.12.1999*. June 20, 2013. http://www.aka.fi/fi/A/Ohjelmat-ja-yhteistyo/Tutkimusohjelmat/Paattyneet/Venajan-ja-Ita-Euroopan-tutkimusohjelma/Seminaari-7121999/Vesa-Saarikoski/.

Sailas, Anne, Susiluoto Ilmari, and Martti Valkonen. 1996. *Jättiläinen tuuliajoilla* [*Giant on Drift*]. Helsinki: Edita.

Statistics of the Finnish Graduate School for Russian and East European Studies, between 1998 and 2012. Archive of the Graduate School (Doctoral Porgram).

Statistics of the Finnish Master's Programme in Russian and East European Studies, between 2005 and 2012. Archive of the Finnish Master's Programme.

Susiluoto, Ilmari. 1997. "Väitöksiä syntyi monta" ["Lots of Doctoral Theses were Produced"]. *Helsingin Sanomat* 13.2.1997.

Szücs, Jenö. 1983. *Vázlat Európa három regiójáról* [*Sketches of the Three Main Regions of Europe*]. Budapest: Magvetö.

Teivainen, Teuvo. 2013. *Teuvo Teivaisen maailmanpoliittiset kävelyt* [*The Walking Tours of Teuvo Teivainen*]. YLE Tiedetoimitus.

The End of the Story? Problems and Perspectives of East European Literary Studies. 2013. Princeton University Workshop, February 8–9, 2013. Organised by Irena Grudzinska Gross, Serguei Oushakine, Andrzej Tymowski, 11 June 2013. http://easteuropeanliterarystudies.wordpress.com.

Tiusanen, Tauno. 2011. *Naurattu sukupolvi. Suomettumisen ilot ja murheet* [*Ridiculed Generation: The Fun and Sadness of Finlandisation*]. Helsinki: Edita.

Vesikansa, Jarkko. 1997. "Venäjä valmiina" ["Russia is Ready"]. *Ylioppilaslehti* 9 (5): 16–17.

THE POLITICS OF EAST EUROPEAN AREA STUDIES

Vihavainen, Timo. 1991. *Kansakunta rähmällään* [*Short History of Finlansiation*]. Keuruu: Suomettumisen lyhyt historia.

Vihavainen, Timo. 1997. "Mitä on suomalainen Venäjän tuntemus ja mihin sitä tarvitaan?" ["What is Finnish Russia-expertise and What Do We Need It For"]. *Idäntutkimus* 2: 50–55.

Yhteishankehaku, Ihmisen mieli. (Suomen Akatemia ja Russian Foundation of Humanities). 2013. 24 June 2013. http://www.aka.fi/fi/A/Tutkijalle/Rahoitusmahdollisu udet/Aakkosjarjestyksessa/Yhteishankehaku-Ihmisen-mieli-Suomen-Akatemia-ja-RFH-Venaja–/.

Yliopistolaki 558/2009. 2009. *Finlex: Lainsäädäntö*. 6 June 2013. http://www.finlex.fi/ fi/laki/alkup/2009/20090558?search[type]=pika&search[pika]=558%2F2009.

Is There Really Something Like "Eastern Europe"? And If So, Why Do We Need Area Studies of It?

Dieter Segert

Eastern Europe is more than only a pure geographical term; it is an invention of the eighteenth century. Later, it became a catchword for the Soviet bloc. The puzzle consists in the fact that it did not disappear after the end-of-state socialism. The paper presents good causes as to why there should be further pursuing of an academic discipline of area studies on Eastern Europe. The thesis will be demonstrated by resuming the discussion about the nature of state socialism.

Eastern Europe can be regarded as a pure geographical term, as the Eastern part of the continent "Europe". But this is not the question the author is mainly interested in at this place. Within the discipline "area studies", the specific space is not determined by geographical borderlines first of all. It is more about imagination. "Eastern Europe" was — as we have learned by Larry Wolff — an invention of the eighteenth century (Wolff 1994). Eastern Europe is additionally determined by a specific economic situation, by its economic backwardness. As Joseph Rothschild and Nancy M. Wingfield pointed out with regard to the situation in the interwar period: "By virtual every relevant statistical index, East Central Europe was less productive, less literate, and less healthy than West Central and Western Europe" (Rothschild and Wingfield 2000, 10–11). Eastern Europe is marked by a certain economic backwardness and by a set of institutions and particular experiences of certain generations with these institutions. For multidisciplinary area studies centred on Eastern Europe, it is a question of practical relevance whether there is a real and consistent topic of research and of education.

THE POLITICS OF EAST EUROPEAN AREA STUDIES

This paper will handle two different problems, connected with the general topic: Firstly, it refers to the German and European debate about the disappearance of a homogeneous Eastern Europe in the last two decades. Secondly, there will be developed some arguments about the feasibility of area studies as a multidisciplinary endeavour using the example of the discussions about the nature of state socialism.

1. On the Reality of Eastern Europe After the End-of-State Socialism

The most widespread topic in the recent German discussion was the question whether Eastern Europe as a specific political-geographic entity has disappeared as a result of the collapse of Soviet state socialism. The historian Jörg Baberowski has provoked much of that discussion with his assumption of the inevitable end of "East European History" as an academic discipline (Baberowski 1998[1]). Later on (in 2003), the German "Deutsche Gesellschaft für Osteuropakunde" (German Association of the Study of Eastern Europe) organized a workshop mainly of political scientists on the same question. In one of the statements, Hans-Henning Schröder (a Historian and Political Analyst of present-day Russia from the think tank SWP in Berlin) stressed the political mandate of the German "Oststudien" (studies on Eastern Europe) in the 1930s. And he saw a kind of continuity in the 1950s and 1960s, in the time period of the cold war, when German Sovietology was a clear weapon within the systemic contestation between West and East. It seems logical from this perspective that at least after 1989, there should be a clear break with this tradition.

Connected to the same discourse, Wolfgang Eichwede (at that time the director of the well-known "Forschungsstelle Osteuropa Bremen") had underlined at the same workshop, that the denomination of his institute was a bit outdated. In his words: "There is no longer a region that could be called Eastern Europe". Scholars from the region would identify themselves as Europeans or Central Europeans but no longer as East Europeans.[2] The only argument against the renaming would be the long "tradition" of the "Forschungsstelle Osteuropa". It is a well-known label that is worthwhile to preserve. In the recent internet appearance of "Forschungsstelle", there is written in this spirit:

> The *Forschungsstelle* — founded in the midst of the Cold War in 1982 — understands itself as an institution which tries to come to terms with the history of the Eastern Bloc and its societies with a particular culture as well as to analyze the transformation and the present situation of successor states.[3]

The debate on the real existence of Eastern Europe in the present is closely connected with the question of post-socialism. Petra Stykow has stated recently (Stykow 2012) that the term post-socialism could be understood as a pure description of the former belonging by certain countries to a lost type of

THE POLITICS OF EAST EUROPEAN AREA STUDIES

society, the state socialist countries, the so-called "Eastern Bloc". In this sense, there is no more "Eastern Europe" today. The ongoing use of Eastern European studies would be regarded from this angle only as a "Post Cold War" phenomenon. But Stykow explained later on that this was only one minor facet of a more comprehensive discussion on post-socialist Eastern Europe.

The topic of "post-socialism" was discovered first by anthropologists working empirically on state socialism already before 1989. Katherine Verdery was probably the most prominent scholar in this group. In her book on socialism and post-socialism in Romania published in 1996, she described her findings as well as her way to the field. Together with her were other scholars like Burawoy and Verdery (1999) or Hann (2002). Many others followed them and the number of publications on post-socialism rose (see among others Berry 2004; Svašek 2005; Brandelj 2008). The term spread as well into the political science debate (Segert 2007; Knobloch 2011; Kollmorgen 2012).

Another conference on the reality of Eastern Europe as a whole was organized by the East Europe Study Group at the Institute for Political Science in Vienna in the year 2006. There was a comprehensive discussion with colleagues from Germany, Austria and several East Central European countries on the topic of "post-socialism".[4] In the centre of the debate on whether the past of post-socialism in Eastern Europe has continued in its present is the question of what kinds of *footprints* are left in the region, as David Lane has asked.[5] Are they only producing troubles in the respective societies or is there any positive heritage also? To quote again this author: "A positive legacy of communism is high investment in human capital which is a considerable asset in the transformation" (Lane 2005, 60). This kind of legacy made it possible that many Western factories could find successful branches in this country right after the end of the old order. This way, Bratislava became a main location for car production in Europe.

The author of this paper would like to add one assumption to the former argument on post-socialism: Eastern Europe as a particular spatial and temporal unit is marked *both* by the legacy of state socialism *and* by a more recent process, namely the deep transformation of the respective societies after 1989/91. Therefore, in my opinion, the present Eastern Europe is marked by those "foot prints of state socialism" *and* by the legacy of – as Kornai named it with regard to the classical book of Karl Polanyi – the "Great Transformation from socialism to capitalism" (Kornai 2006).

There were, therefore, *two* big transformations in Eastern Europe in the twentieth century (Beyme 1994, 70; Segert 2013, 29): The first, the transformation from an early capitalism towards state socialism that started in 1917, and, the second, that started after the break down of this respective society and power structure in 1989/1991. The second was described as the way from socialism to capitalism (or, as Iván T. Berend named it: As a detour from capitalism to capitalism Berend 1996).

In both cases, the legacy of the transformation processes was lasting because of the *traumatic* results of the interconnected changes of the economic, political and social spheres. Important parts of societies have moved either downwards or upwards. The unusual degree and speed of vertical social mobility remained in the memories of the people. It has left a deep mark in the social memory of the respective societies.

There are different reasons for the big emotions: In the case of the transformation during state socialism, the effect was determined by the force used against the "enemy", i.e. the opponents of the new order, especially in the first years of the transformation, just after "Stalinization" started at the end of the 1940s. Secondly, in the case of post-socialist transformation, the outcome was driven by the feeling of betrayed hopes, and of an unjust distribution of the economic wealth among the population. In the latter case, this emotion became very strong approximately 15 years after the starting point in 1989/1990. In East Central and South-eastern Europe, the outburst of emotions came in the so-called "post-accession crisis" in 2005/2006 or 2008/09, respectively (Ehrke 2007; Andreev 2009).

The distinctiveness of Eastern Europe was visible as well in the different impacts of the economic world crisis in the years after 2008. The peripheral capitalisms of Eastern Europe were — as a rule (and with the exception of Poland) — much more affected by this world crisis than the central capitalisms in Western Europe and North America (Compare Segert 2013, 210–214).

The mood within the population changed dramatically within approximately these 15 years. Kornai described it in the following way:

> As the disillusionment over socialism began to take hold, expectations became more pronounced. The hope emerged that a change in the system would resolve all problems, quickly, for everyone. [...] The first great hopes got a cold shower with the serious transformational recession of the 1990s. The people had barely time to recover before new and unrealistic expectations were formed again, this time in regard to membership in the European Union. (Kornai 2006, 235–236)

What are the features of such a double legacy? Firstly, one sign of it is the high degree of frustration within the bulk of the population about their results in most of the countries of EE (see e.g. End of Communism 2009). Another, second legacy consists in deepening social inequality mainly in the societies of South-eastern Europe and the post-Soviet societies. This high degree of inequality is rooted in the privatization processes in the 1990s. The so-called "primitive accumulation"[6] of private capital has left deep traces in Eastern Europe. In a process of appropriation of former state property mainly by a small group of people, a new bourgeoisie has emerged. For the output of these quick and radical privatization processes, it is not the main point whether the new bourgeoisie emerged from the old "nomenklatura" or from the broader society or from the West (see King (2002), and King and Szelényi (2005) on three paths of emerging capitalism in East European and East Asian post-socialism: "capitalism from above", "c. from without", "c. from below"). More important for the legacy of these processes is a widespread feeling of injustice within the bulk of the population that was created by every possible kind of privatization of state property. There was no kind of privatization that was able to solve the problem of injustice.

Up to now, this paper has restricted itself to the state socialist legacy and the legacy of the post-socialist transformation. Is there perhaps still another, deeper impact of the history before state socialism? Some researchers are of this opinion. The Hungarian Economic Historian Iván T. Berend, for instance, has added a third historical stratum: Isn't Eastern Europe different also because of its pre-socialist history? The region was an area of backwardness in Europe long before state socialism, a periphery of its more developed Western and Northern parts (Table 1).

Backwardness is usually regarded as a result of economic dependency. The economic centre of West and north-western Europe has organized for itself a periphery of semi-modernized, semi-traditional societies in the South and the East of Europe. A kind of economic exchange was institutionalized that is favourable mostly for the centre and not for the periphery. This uneven relationship has reproduced the difference in the level of economic development between the West and the East during the nineteenth century and the first half of the twentieth century (Chirot 1989; Berend 1996). But backwardness is much more than just an economic fact. As Berend has expressed it:

> The most characteristic organizational structure, the kinship and networking connections remained an integral part of the social fabric in the region. Modernization initiated changes already in the nineteenth century, urban enclaves exhibited Western characteristics, but social modernization trailed economic development. All of these pre-modern structures of the society were preserved until World War II. (Berend 2007, 277)[7]

However, the question of the real impact of these long-lasting legacies in the present is disputed. There is the controversial argument of Longworth in his well known book of 1992 (The Making of Eastern Europe), that the starting point of Eastern Europe as a particular European region was the partition

Table 1. Development of the gross national product per capita compared to the European average in per cent (Bairoch quoted by Berend 1996, 187)

	Year		
Country	1860	1910	1938
Czechoslovakia	n.k.	98	82
Hungary	74	75	67
Poland	n.k.	(70)	55
Bulgaria	68	55	63
Romania	64	61	51
Yugoslavia	71	56	50

between East and West Rome in the fourth century. Historians like to refer in general to the "longue durée" of certain processes. Another example of this is the explanation of the specific features of Central Europe by Jenö Szücs. In his understanding, East Central Europe as a specific subregion between the West and the East was born in the sixteenth century (Szücs [1983] 1990). Szücs's argument was important for the discussion on "Central Europe" among Polish, Czech and Hungarian intellectuals in 1980s.

But political scientists would like to ask if history is really a destiny, a fate?! The author of this paper has some doubts about these very long shadows of history. History in his opinion is better understood as a sequence of alternatives. Every new generation has the chance to decide by itself which one of the respective alternatives it would like to prefer and then act in this direction more or less successfully. Structures and structural legacies matter, but which one matters depends on decisions of the acting generation.

To sum up this part of the paper: The reality of a common East European space is constituted by the near past that was traumatic for the generations then living. The memory of these generations and their subsequent offspring is the substance that holds Eastern Europe together. Area studies on Eastern Europe are possible and have a real subject because of the social memory of these generations and of the material and cultural remnants of the state socialism and of the transition period afterwards.

2. On the Potential Asset of Multidisciplinary Cooperation Within Area Studies: Several Ways to Interpret "State Socialism"

At the beginning, let me offer some critical considerations on area studies as part of the discipline of Political Science: Stephen A. Hanson wrote about this topic. His paper is part of the *Sage Handbook of Comparative Politics*. At the beginning of his article, he has dealt with three critical arguments against the feasibility of area studies (2009, 161–165). Firstly, "one common criticism of area studies is that its particular orientations and choice of material were directly influenced by the Cold War priorities of the United States government – in particular, the global struggle against communism" (161). A second argument at the expense of area studies consists in the assumption that it "fails to take into account the new social, technological and cultural trends in an area of increasing 'globalisation'"(162). The second argument is connected to the claim that scholars in area studies tend to ignore both the "erosion of state boundaries as a result of cross-border trade, migration, epidemics, and media" and "non state actors ranging from democratic advocacy groups to terrorist cells". Both criticisms were disproved by Hanson through the argument that area specialists are at least no more influenced by the cold war politics and no more ignorant towards new tendencies of globalization than representatives of other approaches. A third critical argument consists in the thesis that area studies "has historically been carried out by scholars resistant to general theoretical concepts and innovative methodologies" (163). Later on in his article, Hanson demonstrated that this counter-argument as a rule stems just from scholars who follow another theoretical paradigm than the respective criticized area researchers. Therefore, their criticism could be regarded less as an argument about a wrong relationship between area analyses and theory *in general* but more as a result of the contest between *different* theoretical approaches with the aim of defeating the other.

In order to prove the potential productivity of area studies on Eastern Europe, the author is going to discuss in the following part of the paper a case study of the way in which the perspectives of different disciplines on state socialism can combine more productively. Area study is a multidisciplinary undertaking. And this multidisciplinarity brings up a certain amount of difficulty.

Why is it so difficult to exceed the limits of one's own scientific discipline? To express it simply: It is not easy to keep up to date in one's own discipline, but it is much more difficult to realize at least the most important upheavals in neighbouring disciplines.

Furthermore, there is a general problem of the inherent dynamics of a scholarly debate: Any scholar tries to defend his own position against the conception of all others. There is the strong need for survival of one's own assumptions in a competition with other arguments. This competition both fosters and hinders the process of cooperation even in the same discipline, and this behavioural pattern causes still more problems in the cooperation with other disciplines.

To go beyond the limits of one's own discipline is difficult as well for a more structural reason. The development of sciences went in just the contrary direction, the way of an increasing division of labour. Sciences are to be understood as specialized perspectives on a single real object. These perspectives are organized through certain theoretical assumptions and special methods plus a special way of posing questions. The driving forces of these practices of cognition and specialized sign systems are twofold, both endogenous scientific and practical. The endogenous driving forces are problems that should be solvable within the framework of specific paradigms. The practical reasons for scientific advancement become visible in the fact that during a certain period of time it is always the case that a certain discipline is the most accepted. It enjoys the most public attention and financial support. And in another time period, some other discipline gets the desired position. Engels (1894) wrote in a letter to a contemporary: "If society has a technical need that helps science forward more than ten universities."

To develop this historical argument a bit further: The science of history received considerable impetus from the national revival movements and the secular national states in the nineteenth century. Connected to planning processes within Western states between the Second World War and the 1970s, several social sciences like urban sociology and demography were in rising demand. In the age of discovery, cartography and navigation were developed.

The natural sciences were pushed forward by the industrial revolution in which new scientific knowledge opened up new kinds of production with new chances of high profits. The "zeitgeist" plays an important role by boosting one or another science or art.

The main trend of the Modern Age is the radical differentiation of sciences, the increase of faculties from the classical 4 (Theology, Philosophy, Law and Medicine) to 15 and more. The increasing division of labour in sciences has many advantages, but disadvantages as well. This way, one learns more and more precisely about ever less. Highly developed differentiation of knowledge production needs synthesis, especially for the practical use of knowledge. This combination and merging of different sciences and arts is an additional scholarly task by itself. It is realized by "applied sciences". Area studies on Eastern Europe are in this sense an "applied science" too.

Area studies of Eastern Europe were first of all characterized by a focus on a certain social and geographical space. The combination of insights, theories and methods, from different arts and social sciences on this space in order to get practical, usable knowledge was seen as the aim. But to formulate the task is easier than to realize it. The necessity to become an expert in one's own discipline hampers the ability to look beyond the edge of this discipline. Only then, if every participant in the cooperation is able to look beyond their own nose does the synthesis become possible.

The following text contains a general problem combined with a personal narrative: The author's interest in the debate on the nature of state socialism was firstly pushed by an emotional aversion to the dominant discussion on the topic. He learned by reading the Western books on history of this society after 1989 (when he first got the opportunity to do so) that there was a revival of the concept of totalitarianism on the way both in History and in Political Science. But his opinion, both as a citizen of the late socialist GDR and as a reform socialist in the last years of the respective state, pushed him forward in his criticism of the concept of totalitarian rule. His first argument at that time was to underline the difference between high Stalinism and the late socialist societies. He developed this point in several publications over the years (Compare Segert and Machos 1995; Segert 1998; Segert 2002, chaps. 4 and 5).

But, after a while the author had to admit also that his first attempt to develop the topic was not well balanced enough. His first counter-arguments against the hegemonic discourse, against the *zeitgeist,* were a bit too sharp, too polemical. It reminds us of the way in which Louis Althusser (1976, 71) defined the task of militant philosophy: to turn the bent nail in the other direction. The "catch-up modernization" became the key word. Against the belief of an omnipotent state (in the concept of totalitarianism), the conception of limits of power was put by him. Against the conception of the exclusive power of the high echelon of the elite, the author started to stress the interaction between elite and sub-elite (the "service class" of state socialism, Segert 2009b).

THE POLITICS OF EAST EUROPEAN AREA STUDIES

The more balanced answer was in a new term, the differentiation of power relations in state socialism: The state socialist power relation consists of three elements, the political elite, the sub-elites and a certain degree of acceptance of the system by a broader public. The state socialist dictatorship can only be understood as a modern one (in the sense of Max Weber's "legitimate authority"); which denotes that this kind of power needs support from the side of the subjects. In this direction went another argument: state socialism was more than just a *political* regime (totalitarian dictatorship) — it was a *social* system too (Segert 2009a, 413).

But again the self-criticism of the author follows. Area studies on state socialism would have need of a more balanced use of arguments. The main point should be: How to combine the divergent perspectives on the common object (East European state socialism) in a productive way? Every conception has *both* a certain potential of cognition *and* certain limits. Only a synthesis of different approaches with their respective perspectives and assumptions delivers the needed result. From the point of view of area studies, the combination of different approaches hits the spot. That became clear over the years.

What can be learned for a more general understanding of area studies on Eastern Europe by that personal way of coming to terms with state socialism? Instead of searching for an exclusively right conception or interpretation in area studies, one should better look for a mosaic of different insights into the same subject. No single model has the potential to explain alone the whole political-geographical region of Eastern Europe and its main developments. The model of a "catch-up modernization" and the idea connected with that term of a "modernising dictatorship" could explain a good deal of the social developments in Eastern Europe after 1917 (or 1945). These assumptions enable the posing of interesting research questions such as: Was the catch-up modernization of Eastern European countries only a less effective way towards the same Western type of modern society or was it another way to modernity? Why did the success of this modernization end just in the middle of the 1970s (Berend 1996, 222)? What was the impact of the political system of state socialism on the deficit of its economic success?

Regardless of its explanatory potential, the conception of "catch-up modernization" has several blind spots too: The high degree of centralization of decision power and of force in the political system of early state socialism could not be understood by the model of a rational means of forced modernization. It retains a good deal of irrationalism and destruction within it. But another counter-argument consists in the fact that the model of "catch-up modernization" is just as unable to explain another feature of the history of state socialism, namely that state socialism was not by intention only a system of forced modernization. It was also a programme for a "better society" compared to the existing capitalism of that time. The reform socialist current in state socialist societies cannot be described without the utopia of a just and free society. The biography of people like Imre Nagy, Alexander Dubček or Michael Gorbachev or of the socialist-communist dissidents like Robert

Havemann or Andréj Sákharov cannot fully be understood through analysis of a society that fought only against the backwardness of its respective position in relation to the West.

Political scientists should explain first of all the functioning of political rule in state socialist societies. At first we can start with the model of "totalitarian dictatorship" (Arendt 1955; Friedrich and Brzezinski 1956; and some newer authors: Arnason 1993; Brie 1996; Linz and Stepan 1996). It expresses successfully, the comprehensive claims of the traditional communist elite groups towards their societies. Certain institutions have embodied this claim to a great extent (like the all-embracing practice of secret police in countries like the Soviet Union, the GDR or Romania).

But this conception has serious disadvantages as well. It simplifies the way of ruling, underrates especially the interaction of the elite with the service class and the mass of the population. Walter Süß has detected the dependency of the GDR state security on the support of the bulk of the rank and file in the communist SED. He can explain through this the miracle of why a mighty institution was so powerless and inactive during the fall of 1989 (Süß 1999). The embeddedness of the dictatorship within society is able to explain the changes in the type of state socialism in its last decades. The emergence of "consumer socialism" (Staritz 1996) in some of the countries of East Central Europe could be explained by the social embeddedness of the political power relations.

But this perspective is limited too. The changes described were not the result of a "social contract" (Cook 1993) because in this kind of society there was no negotiation between the power elite and the subjects, except at some rare moments in Polish history (after Gierek came to power or in the summer of 1980) or in the late perestroika under Gorbachev. It was more a result of adaptation of the elite to non-public signals from below.

Within state socialist systems, the informal plays a decisive role. Analyses of political scientists "on the transformation of politics in post-communism still lacks a more precise picture of [...] how informal mechanisms influence political decision making" (Meyer 2008, 15). But cultural and ethnographic studies have tried successfully to reconstruct the day-to-day behaviour of ordinary people and of the subtle changes in their perception of the socialist ruling order. A well-known book by Yurchak (2006) on the last Soviet generation of youth functionaries in St. Petersburg explains to a great extent the paradoxes within the behaviour of members of the lower sub-elite just before and after the end of the Soviet Union. Yurchak is able to explain both the stability and the sudden end of the loyalty of these people. He studied a group of people which originally held the opinion that socialism would be a kind of eternal state but suddenly and most surprisingly they had the intuition that it would definitely collapse. And after 1991, he observed the paradox that the new and very different society that emerged in Russia after the end of the Soviet Union found them well prepared for the changes. For the most part of the 300 pages of his study, Yurchak is trying to explain these

THE POLITICS OF EAST EUROPEAN AREA STUDIES

paradoxes. One of his main theses consists in the following: Under the cover of the late socialist-collectivist political rituals a culture emerged that gave much space for individual differences of lifestyle and interest. By performing these meaningless public rituals the last Soviet generation produced its own personal meanings and in doing so they prepared themselves for the future life in post-Soviet capitalism.

So far to the advantages of this kind of study but it has as well a clear limit. Yurchak has distinguished his own position clearly from the totalitarian approach. But due to his conception of change, he is unable to recognize the achievements of the reformers with regard to the changes. The reformers were regarded by him as "activists" who were taking the official discourse at face value. The same ignorance is visible via the dissidents: Activists and dissidents were both pictured as people who are marginalised and could not influence the changes in late socialism. That blind spot is caused by his discourse-analytical approach. Late socialism is characterized mainly by the authoritative discourse in his opinion. Consequently, Yurchak put his main emphasis on the processes of *de-ideologization* of the official (authoritative) discourse. Both the "activists" and the "dissidents" are characterized as agents that do not notice this important "performative trend". They tend to act *as if* the former official ideology still would matter for anybody.[8]

In the Yurchakian model of interpretation, only the high echelon of the party elite (Gorbachev) was able to change the authoritative discourse (Yurchak 2006, 292 et seq.). From this author's point of view, however the reformers and the dissidents executed much more influence on the changing interpretations of politics and society and — connected with that — they influenced as well the change in the whole "authoritative discourse" in late socialism over the years.

And now to a last piece of the mosaic: The conception of transnational actors (Tarrow 2005; Brier 2011). Interesting questions were posed within the framework of this conception too: How were intellectuals in Eastern and Western Europe interconnected with each other and what was the impact of their interaction on the changes in Eastern Europe? To what degree were the neoliberal politics in the East influenced by transnational networks situated in the West? (See Bohle and Neunhöffer Bohle and Neunhöffer 2007). However, a blind spot of these analyses of transnational actors remains the structural change caused by economic trends; in other words, it is the framework that determines the real scope of the behaviour of actors.

To sum up at the end: Area studies of Eastern Europe with its multidisciplinary perspective are able to reproduce the necessary mosaic of important facts and trends in the region during the state socialist time period. Unlike single disciplines area studies should not struggle mainly to confirm or refute one or another competitive conception of subjects of research. Their aim is to produce verifiable knowledge about practically important problems. With their help, it should be possible better to understand the societies of Eastern Europe. Area studies aim to develop practice-relevant insights on the countries of the region. At least this is the case when the topic is the present. If — as in the case of our example — the area studies have dealt with the past, then it remains their advantage to be able to combine the theories and methods of several disciplines (History, Political Science, Linguistics, Ethnology, Cultural Studies) in order to gain a complex and comprehensive picture of whole societies.

3. Some Concluding Reflections on the Time Frame of "Postsocialism"

In Hanson's quoted article, there was an easy but fundamental question posed: "What is in an area?" (Hanson 2009, 165). Hanson stressed the somehow arbitrary nature of regional borderlines. The whole discussion may be attributed to the simple question of whether the borderlines of certain areas like Eastern Europe are simply "arbitrary" or rather not. This article has already pointed to Larry Wolff and the invention of Eastern Europe in the enlightenment. There is still more evidence of the possible dependence of regional characteristics on mental maps. One of them is the debate on the interpretations of the "Balkans" by Maria Todorova (1997). Another one is the well-known discussion on "Central Europe" in the second half of the 1980s that was conducted by intellectuals from the East Central European countries (Segert 2002, chap. 1.2).

But is the demarcation really only "arbitrary"? If the state socialist legacy and the legacy of the radical transformation processes might lie at the ground of the particular nature of Eastern Europe then there could be another answer to the question of what an area is. It is not about a reason that is valid for ever; it is about *how long* the respective heritage is valid. I quote again Hanson: "Indeed, certain geographical zones that appear to be 'regions' in one historical period can suddenly lose their apparent cohesiveness in another" (166).

Petra Stykow has connected the existence of Eastern Europe with the existence of the phenomenon of post-socialism. "Most authors are of the opinion that the effects of state socialism will still serve as a point of reference for a certain period of time, it will serve therefore as a context for the individuals and public constructions of reality" (Stykow 2012, 8). The author would like to add: The state socialist impression is connected in Eastern Europe as well with the experience of the radical transformation processes in the 1990s.

At the end only two reflections:

Firstly, on the possible timeframe of post-socialist Eastern Europe: If the demarcations of areas are closely bound to common interpretations of experiences than it could be expected that a new generation would construct the area in a new way. Certainly, the collective memory of a generation is interlinked with cultural memory. That is visible from the politics of history circle in Poland for example when in 2005 a new wave of politics of history was elevating. The government led by the Kaczynski brothers and the PiS party has tried to mobilize its constituency by the narrative that ordinary Poles were betrayed by the round table talks in 1989 and by a coalition of "communists and liberals" since then. The answer they gave was the so called "Fourth

THE POLITICS OF EAST EUROPEAN AREA STUDIES

Republic". There is additionally a process of passing of values and experience from the former to the next generation. The children of a generation of traumatized parents will reproduce their emotional balances. But nevertheless, at a certain point of time the foot prints of state socialism and of transformation will become less visible. There is no doubt about this.

When will that point of return be arrived? In my opinion, the generation groups that were born between 1945 and 1975 were the main agency of socialist, post-socialist and transformation experience. They are the population of a common Eastern Europe in the present. If and when these groups disappear the existence of a clear cut area of Eastern Europe could again be questioned.

Secondly, there remain some additional questions: The political culture of some of the East European countries (in the Eastern and the Southern parts of the region) is marked by the particularity of Christian Orthodoxy. In Bulgaria 60% of population declared their affiliation to the Orthodox Church. In Romania feel even nearly 90% affiliated to that, in Serbia 85%. In Russia, this group is much smaller, namely 20%. But the influence of religion and church is not identical with these figures. In the present, the influence of the church in the day-to-day life of the people is not overwhelming but maybe there will be a renaissance of it in the future?

A last topic concerns the fact that the state socialist institutional order was not restricted to Eastern Europe. In that sense the foot prints of state socialism are not restricted to those societies. To pose it that way: Could we have post-socialist studies in countries outside of Eastern Europe? State socialist institutional orders were existent in five countries of East Asia (China, North Korea, Vietnam, Laos and Kampuchea) or Cuba in Latin America as well. In these cases, a certain institutional order but not a regional assignment were the basis for "areas" related to the study of comparative politics, to quote Stykow again (2012, 13—14). The regional comparison would aim to study the traces that a certain institutional order (party-state-state economics) has produced after its very end. Finally, if the area "Eastern Europe" as a whole were to disappear there could be other regional aspects which would survive instead: e.g. the Baltic Sea region or the Black Sea region. The productivity of multidisciplinary area studies at least would have a good chance to outlast the disappearance of Eastern Europe.

Notes

1. See for the whole of the discussion in the journal "Osteuropa" the volume edited by Creuzberger u.a. (2000).
2. Compare Attila Ágh (1998): He has differentiated between Central Europe, Southeastern Europe and the "proper Eastern Europe"; the latter is identical with the successor states of Soviet Union minus the Baltic States.
3. See: http://www.forschungsstelle.uni-bremen.de/ (the text is originally written in German, read at November 15, 2012, translation into English by D.S.).

THE POLITICS OF EAST EUROPEAN AREA STUDIES

4. The results of the conference were published in a book by the Vienna publishing house Braumüller (Segert 2007.)
5. The term "footprint" was coined by David Lane (2005, 48).
6. See the Marxian term "ursprüngliche Akkumulation des Kapitals" in "Das Kapital", vol. 1, chap. 23 (Marx 1967).
7. The question remains whether and if so to which degree the state socialist modernization was able to override the backwardness. But the answer could be given only in empirical analyses.
8. Compare Yurchak, chapter "Activists, dissidents and *svoi*" (2006, 102–108).

References

Ágh, Attila. 1998. *The Politics of Central Europe*. London: Sage.

Althusser, Louis. 1976. "Reply to John Lewis." In *Essays in Self-Criticism*, Translated and edited by Grahame Lock, 34–77. London: New Left Books.

Andreev, Svetlozar A. 2009. *Is Populism the "Bad Wolf"? Post-accession Crisis of Representative Democracy in Bulgaria and Romania*. Aberdeen, SD: Centre for the Study of Public Policy.

Arendt, Hannah. 1955. *Elemente und Ursprünge Totaler Herrschaft* [*The Origins of Totalitarianism*]. Frankfurt a.M.: Büchergilde Gutenberg.

Arnason, Johann P. 1993. *The Future that Failed Origins and Destinies of the Soviet Model*. London: Routledge.

Baberowski, Jörg. 1998. "Das Ende der Osteuropäischen Geschichte. Bemerkungen zur Lage einer geschichtswissenschaftlichen Disziplin" ["The End of the East European History. Comments on the State of the Art in a Sub-discipline of the Science of History"]. *Osteuropa* 48 (8/9): S784–S799.

Berend, Ivan T. 1996. *Central and Eastern Europe, 1944–1993: Detour from the Periphery to the Periphery*. Cambridge: Cambridge University Press.

Berend, Ivan T. 2007. "Social Shock in Transforming Central and Eastern Europe." *Communist and Post-Communist Studies* 40 (3): 269–280.

Berry, Chris. 2004. *Postsocialist Cinema in Post-Maoist China: The Cultural Revolution after the Cultural Revolution*. New York: Routledge.

von Beyme, Klaus. 1994. *Systemwechsel in Osteuropa* [*Systemic change in Eastern Europe*]. Frankfurt a.M.: Suhrkamp-Taschenbuch Wissenschaft 1130.

Bohle, Dorothee, and Gisela Neunhöffer. 2007. "Why Is There No Third Way? The Role of Neoliberal Ideology, Networks and Think-tanks in Combating Market Socialism and Shaping Transformation in Poland." In *Neoliberal Hegemony: A Global Critique*, edited by D. Plehwe, B. Walpen, and G. Neunhöffer, 89–105. Vol. 18. London: Routledge (RIPE Series in Global Political Economy 18).

Brandelj, Nina. 2008. *From Communists to Foreign Capitalists: The Socials Foundations of Foreign Direct Investment in Postsocialist Europe*. Princeton, NJ: Princeton University Press.

Brie, Michael. 1996. "Staatssozialistische Länder Europas im Vergleich" ["State Socialist Countries of Europe in Comparison"]. In *Einheit als Privileg. Vergleichende Perspektiven auf die Transformation Ostdeutschlands* [*Unification as Privilege. Comparative Perspectives in the Transformation of Eastern Germany*], edited by H. Wiesenthal, 39–104. Frankfurt a.M.: Campus.

Brier, Robert. 2011. "Adam Michnik's Understanding of Totalitarianism and the West European Left: A Historical and Transnational Approach to Dissident Political Thought." *East European Politics and Societies* 25 (2): 197–218.

Burawoy, Michael, and Katherine Verdery, eds. 1999. *Uncertain Transition: Ethnographies of Change in Postsocialist World*. Lanham: Rowman & Littlefield.

THE POLITICS OF EAST EUROPEAN AREA STUDIES

Chirot, Daniel. 1989. *The Origins of Backwardness in Eastern Europe: Economics and Politics from the Middle Ages until the Early Twentieth Century.* Conference papers, edited by D. Chirot. Berkeley: University of California Press.

Cook, Linda J. 1993. *The Social Contract and Why It Failed: Welfare Policy and Workers' Politics from Brezhnev to Yeltsin.* Cambridge, MA: Harvard University Press.

Creuzberger u.a., Stephan (Hrsg.) 2000. *Wohin Steuert Die Osteuropaforschung? Eine Diskussion* [*Whereto goes the research on Eastern Europe? A controversy*]. Köln: Verlag Wissenschaft und Politik.

Ehrke, Michael. 2007. *Ungarische Unruhen — ein Symptom der zentraleuropäischen Beitrittskrise?* [*Hungarian unrest — A symptom for the accession crisis in Central Europe?*] FES: Internationale Politik und Gesellschaft Online 2007/1.

End of Communism. 2009. "End of Communism Cheered but Now with More Reservations, Opinion Poll of the Pew Global Attitudes Project." Released November 2, 2009. Accessed February 23, 2013. http://www.pewglobal.org/2009/11/02/end-of-communism-cheered-but-now-with-more-reservations/

Engels, Frederic. 1894. "Letter to Borgius, January 1894." In *Marx & Engels Internet Archive/Marx-Engels Correspondence 1894.* Accessed February 23, 2013. http://www.marxists.org/archive/marx/works/1894/letters/94_01_25.htm

Friedrich, Carl Joachim (with Zbiegniew Brzezinski). 1957. *Totalitäre Diktatur* [*Totalitarian Dictatorship and Autocracy*]. Stuttgert: Kohlhammer.

Hann, Chris. 2002. *Postsocialism: Ideals, Ideologies and Practices in Eurasia.* London: Routledge.

Hanson, Stephen E. 2009. "The Contribution of Area Studies." In *The Sage Handbook of Comparative Politics*, edited by Todd Landman and Neil Robinson, 159—174. Los Angeles.

King, Lawrence. 2002. "Postcommunist Divergence: A Comparative Analysis of Transition to Capitalism in Poland and Russia." *Studies in Comparative International Development* 37 (Fall): 3—34.

King, Lawrence, and Iván Szelényi. 2005. "Post-communist Economic Systems." In *The Handbook of Economic Sociology*, edited by Neil J. Smelser, 205—232. Princeton, NJ: Princeton University Press.

Knobloch, Jörn. 2011. "Postdemokratie und Postsozialismus. Zur Konvergenz zweier Krisen am Beispiel Russlands" ["Postdemocracy and Post-socialism. On the Convergence of two crises using the example of Russia"]. In *Herausforderungen und Gefährdungen der Demokratie durch neue Bedingungen und Akteurinnen* [*Challenge and Endangering of Democracy by New Conditions and New Agents*]. Themenheft [special issue of] der Österreichischen Zeitschrift für Politikwissenschaft, edited by Ulrich Brand et al. 39 (2): 169—182.

Kollmorgen, Raj. 2012. "Anfang vom Ende oder Ende des Anfangs? Zum Stand der transformationstheoretischen Debatte über den Postsozialismus" ["The Start of the Final Stage or the End of the Initial Stage? The State of the Art of the Discussion about Post-socialism"]. In *Osteuropa als Herausforderung: Forschung zwischen Area Studies und Mainstream* [*Eastern Europe as a challenge: Research between Area Studies and Mainstream: Honorary Publication for Melanie Tartur*], edited by Kerstin Zimmer S15—S42. Stuttgart: Ibidem.

Kornai, János. 2006. "The Great Transformation of Central and Eastern Europe. Success and Disappointment." *Economics of Transition* 14 (2): 207—244.

Lane, David. 2005. "Russia's Asymetric Capitalism in Comparative Perspective." In *How to Explain Russia's post-Soviet Political and Economic System?* edited by Heiko Pleines, 46—60. Bremen: Forschungsstelle Osteuropa [Research Institute on Eastern Europe].

Linz, Juan J., and Alfred Stepan. 1996. *Problems of Democratic Transition and Consolidation in Southern Europe, South America, and Post-communist Europe*. Baltimore, MD: Johns Hopkins University Press.

Marx, Karl. 1967. "Das Kapital. Zur Kritik der Politischen Ökonomie, Band 1" ["Capital. A Critique of Political Economy. Vol. 1"]. In *Marx-Engels Werke, Band 23*. Berlin: Dietz.

Meyer, Gerd. 2008. "Formal and Informal Politics: Questions, Concepts and Subjects." In *Formal Institutions and Informal Politics Informal Politics in Central and Eastern Europe*, edited by Gerd Meyer, 15–142. Opladen & Farmington Hill: Barbara Budrich.

Rothschild, Joseph, and Nancy M. Wingfield. 2000. *Return to Diversity. A Political History of East Central Europe Since World War II*. 3rd ed. Oxford: Oxford University Press.

Segert, Dieter, Machos Csilla. 1995. *Parteien in Osteuropa - Kontext und Akteure* [*Parties in Eastern Europe – Actors and Framework*]. Opladen: Westdeutscher Verlag.

Segert, Dieter. 1998. "Was war die DDR? Schnitte durch ihr politisches System" ["What was the GDR? Different Perspectives on Its Political System"]. *Berliner Debatte Initial* 2–3: 5–21.

Segert, Dieter. 2002. *Die Grenzen Osteuropas. 1918, 1945, 1989 – Drei Versuche im Westen anzukommen* [Borderlines/Limits of Eastern Europe. 1918, 1945, 1989 – Three Attempts to Catch-up with the West]. Frankfurt a.M.: Campus.

Segert, Dieter, ed. 2007. *Postsozialismus: Hinterlassenschaften des Staatssozialismus und neue Kapitalismen in Europa* [*Post Socialism: Legacies of State Socialism and new Capitalisms in Europe*]. Wien: Braumüller.

Segert, Dieter. 2009a. "Der Staatssozialismus war mehr als nur ein politisches Herrschaftsverhältnis Anmerkungen zu einem theoretischen Defizit des Totalitarismuskonzepts" ["State Socialism was not only a Political Regime. A Comment on the Concept of Totalitarianism"]. *Bohemia* 49 (2/2010): 412–420. (auf Tschechisch abgedruckt unter dem Titel "Státní socialismus nebyl jen politický mocenský vztah" - in Soudobé Dějniy 4/2009, 709-718.)

Segert, Dieter. 2009b. "The GDR Intelligentsia and Its Forgotten Role During the *Wende* of 1989." *Debatte: Journal of Contemporary Central and Eastern Europe* 17 (2): 143–157.

Segert, Dieter. 2013. *Transformationen in Osteuropa im 20. Jahrhundert* [*Transformation Processes in Eastern Europe in the 20th Century*]. Wien: UTB/Facultas.

Staritz, Dietrich. 1996. *Geschichte der DDR* [History of GDR]. Frankfurt a.M.: Suhrkamp.

Stykow, Petra. 2012. "Postsozialismus" ["Post socialism"], in "Docupedia-Zeitgeschichte." Accessed November 15, 2013. http://docupedia.de/zg/Postsozialismus

Süß, Walter. 1999. *Staatssicherheit am Ende. Warum es den Mächtigen nicht gelang, 1989 Eine Revolution zu verhindern* [*State Security at the End. Why it Was Not Possible For the Power Holder to Avoid a Revolution*]. Berlin: Ch. Links.

Svašek, Maruška. 2005. *Postsocialism: Politics and Emotions in Central and Eastern Europe*. New York: Berghahn Books.

Szücz, Jenö. 1990. *Die drei historischen Regionen Europas* [*The Three Historical Regions of Europe; the Original Hungarian Publication is from 1983*]. Frankfurt a.M.: Neue Kritik.

Tarrow, Sidney. 2005. *The New Transnational Activism*. Cambridge: Cambridge University Press.

Todorova, Marija. 1997. *Imagining the Balkans*. New York: Oxford University Press.

Verdery, Katherine. 1996. *What Was Socialism, and What Comes Next?* Princeton, NJ: Princeton University Press.

Wolff, Larry. 1994. *Inventing Eastern Europe: The Map of Civilization in the Mind of the Enlightment*. Standford, CA: Stanford University Press.

Yurchak, Alexei. 2006. *Everything Was Forever, Until It Was No More: The Last Soviet Generation*. Princeton, NJ: Princeton University Press.

Index

Note: Page numbers in *italic* type refer to tables
Page numbers followed by 'n' refer to notes

actors 89; economic 65-8, 71; non state 84; political 65; rational 14; transnational 89
Africa 21
Ágh, A. 91n
agnosticism 20
Albania 12, 32
Aleksanteri Institute (Russia) 65-8, 71
Alexander I, Tsar of Russia 61
Althusser, L. 86
Anderson, P. 1, 11
Anievas, A.: and Nisancioglu, K. 2
anti-austerity 49-51
anti-fascism 57n
anti-Semitism 8, 17
Asia 2, 7-10, 15, 21, 91
Asmuth, L. 71
austerity 5, 8, 27-8, 32, 47, 51-5, 57n; anti- 49-51; economic 27; fiscal 28
Austria 17, 30, 81; Vienna 2, 92n
authoritarianism 8, 16, 48-50
autonomy 47
Azerbaijan 15

Baberowski, J. 80
Bäckman, J. 69
Balkan Peninsula 7-42
Balkan setbacks (since 2009) 31-3
barbarism 9
Barroso, J.M. 51, 55
Baschmakoff, N. 63
Băsescu, T. 49, 55
Belgium 13
Belorussia 71
Berend, I.T. 83
Bideleux, R. 1, 4-5, 7-42; and Jeffries, I. 18
Birmingham Centre of Russian and East European Studies (UK) 67

Bohemia 9
Bosnia 8, 27, 32
Brandt, W. 31
Budapest 3
Bulgaria 12, 26-7, 33, 47, 91
Burawoy, M.: and Verdery, K. 81

Cameron, D. 47
Cannadine, D. 10
capitalism 2-3, 20, 48, 52-4, 81-2; global 51; neoliberal 27, 34; Western 56n
centralization 67, 87
China 11, 70
Christendom 2, 10-11
Cistelecan, A. 1, 43-58
civil society 22-3, 52-3
class 43-58; struggle 43-5, 56, 57n ; working 55, 57n
Coca-colonization 20
Cold War 15-21, 43, 59-64, 70, 80, 84
collectivism 14, 57n; ethnic 18
colonialism 12, 19, 24, 54
Comisso, E.: and Gutierrez, B. 18
communism 8, 81-4; post- 88
communist bloc 17, 20
communist regimes 8, 21-2
communist states 7, 13-15; post- 8-9, 17-27, 31-4
conservatism 47
consumer socialism 88
consumerism 20-1
continental map 43-5
Crimea 9
Crimean War (1853-6) 3
Croatia 8, 26, 32-3
Cuba 91
cultural differences 46-7
cultural essentialism 5, 15
cultural identity 1, 5, 48

INDEX

cultural stereotyping 11
cultural veil 54-6
culturalism 44-55
culturalization 43-6, 55
culture 43-58
Culture Matters 15
Czech Republic 8, 30-1; Prague 3
Czechoslovakia 12, 31

Dale, G.: Miklóssy, K. and Segert, D. 1-6
Darwinism: social 55, 57n
de-ideologization 89
de-orientalization 4, 7-42
decentralization 28
Delaisi, F. 11
demi-orientalization 9-13
democracy 5, 48-53, 57n, 71; liberal 43, 46; political 53
democratization 25, 30, 35, 73
demoralization 35
Denmark 9, 25
diaspora 31
dichotomy 11-15; East-West 19
dictatorship 88
diplomacy 23
discrimination 25, 45; non- 25
Dubček, A. 87
Duchêne, F. 22-4

East 2-5, 47-50, 64-6, 70-1, 83, 89
East-West dichotomy 19
Eastern Bloc 62, 80-1
economic actors 65-8, 71
economic austerity 27
economic crisis (2008-9) 30
economic growth 5, 8, 26-34
economic liberalization 21-2, 30-3
Economist, The 16
economization 60
economy: political 47-8
education: research-based (Finland) 67-9
Eichwede, W. 80
eighteenth century 3, 7-9, 17, 60, 79
emigration 33, 50
empowerment 4
Engels, F. 11, 85
England 3
enlightenment 9-10, 90
equality: gender 22, 25; racial 25
essentialism 5, 8, 15; cultural 5, 15
essentialization 14
Estonia 27
étatism 14
ethnic collectivism 18
ethnic nationalism 13
ethnicity 12, 25
ethnocracy 12, 25

ethnography 4, 59
Eurasia 1, 70
Euro 34
Euroization 33
Europe 1-4, 7-21, 26-8, 43-52, 71-2, 79-83; Ottoman 9
European Communities (EC) 23-4
European Parliament (EP) 28
European Project 45-9
European Union (EU) 1, 20-34, 47-54, 56-7n, 63-7, 71-4, 82
Europeanism 53
Europeanization 21, 50
Europhobia 29
Euroscepticism 29
Eurozone 7-8, 27-34; crisis (2010-13) 32
Eyal, G.: Szelenyi, I. and Townsley, E. 52

Farage, N. 55
fascism 5, 8, 17-19; anti- 57n
fifteenth century 10
Financial Times, The 16
Finland 59-74; University of Helsinki 61, 72, 75n
Finlandization 69, 72, 74n; post- 69
fiscal austerity 28
Fleming, K.E. 56n
foreign direct investment (FDI) 8, 16, 26-7, 30-3
fourth century 84
France 31
Frank, A.G. 46
Fukuyama, F. 15

Galway (Ireland) 5
Geertz, C. 12
Gellner, E. 12
gender equality 22, 25
Genghis Khan 21
genocide 5, 13
Germany 13, 17, 26-7, 30-1, 56-7n, 81; Merkel 47, 51
global capitalism 51
globalization 4, 84
Gorbachev, M. 16-17, 87-8
Greece 5, 48, 57n
gross national product (GNP) *83*
Guizot, F. 11
Gutierrez, B.: and Comisso, E. 18

Hague, The 23
Häikiö, M. 69
Hann, C. 81
Hanson, S.A. 84-5, 90
Harrison, L. 15
Havel, V. 16-17
Havemann, R. 87-8
Hayek, F. 27

INDEX

hedonism 20
Heinonen, O.-P. 64
Hobson, J.M. 10
Hofstede, G. 15
Holocaust 17
Homo Sovieticus (Zinoviev) 14-15
human rights 3, 22, 66, 73
Hungary 2, 8-9, 12, 29-31, 47
Huntington, S. 15

ICT (information and communications technology) 21
ideology 52; monetarist 52; political 52
Iivonen, J. 63
immigration 55
imperialism 24
India 11
individualism 12-14
integration: stalled 34-5; transformative impacts of European 22-6
internalization 49
Invention of Eastern Europe, The (Wolff) 7
investment: foreign direct (FDI) 8, 16, 26-7, 30-3
Ireland 3, 5, 25
Italy 1, 5, 31, 84

Jaszi, O. 11
Jeffries, I.: and Bideleux, R. 18
Josefstadt (Vienna) 3
Jussila, O. 63

Kagan, R. 23
Kaiwar, V.: Labica, T. and Mazumdar, S. 10
Kekkonen, U. 62
Keyserling, H. 56n
Kirkinen, H. 63
Kivikari, U. 71
Kivinen, M. 67
Kohn, H. 12
Kosovo 27, 32

Labica, T.: Mazumdar, S. and Kaiwar, V. 10
Lane, D. 81, 92n
Lapavitsas, C. 56n
Latin America 21, 91
Latvia 27
Ledeneva, A. 15
Lehti, M. 71
Leonardi, R.: *et al.* 15
Lewis, B. 15
liberal democracy 43, 46
liberalization 35; economic 21-2, 30-3
Lipponen, P. 64
Lithuania 15, 27

London (UK) 3
Luxembourg 23

McCarthy, T. 10
McDonaldization 20
Macedonia 8, 27, 32
Machtpolitik (power politics) 5
macro-regions 15-16
Manners, I. 23-4
marginalization 17, 66
marketization 30-3
Marx, K. 11
Marxism 44
materialism 20, 48
Matthews, B.J. 15
Mazumdar, S.: Kaiwar, V. and Labica, T. 10
Mehta, U. 2
Merkel, A. 47, 51
Miklóssy, K. 1, 4-5, 59-78; Segert, D. and Dale, G. 1-6
Mitrany, D. 11
modernity 45-6, 53, 87; pre- 46
modernization 3, 83-7, 92n
Moldova 71
monetarism 52
monetarist ideology 52
Mongol Empire 2, 21
Monnet, J. 22
Montenegro 8, 27, 32
Montesquieu 11
morality 48
moralization 45
Moscow (Russia) 5
multiculturalism 22, 47
multidisciplinarity 59
multilateralism 23
Muslims 10
Mustajoki, A. 63
mystification 46

Nagy, I. 87
Nanetti, R.Y.: *et al.* 15
nation building 2, 61
nation states 4, 12, 23-5, 59
nationalism 12-13, 19; ethnic 13; ultra- 5, 17-19
NATO (North Atlantic Treaty Organization) 11, 17
Nazism 17
neoliberal capitalism 27, 34
neoliberalism 47
neologism 9
New Russia 63-9
nineteenth century 3, 7, 10, 17, 74, 83-5
Nisancioglu, K.: and Anievas, A. 2
Nissinen, M. 71
non-discrimination 25
non-state actors 84

INDEX

Odom, W. 17
OEEC (Organization for European Economic Co-operation) 11, 20
Orban, V. 31, 47-50
Oriental despotism 7, 10
orientalism 4, 9, 12, 18, 54
orientalization 2, 7-42; de- 7-42; demi- 9-13
Other 4
Otherness 74
Ottoman Europe 9

Paasikivi, J.K. 62
Peltonen, H. 68
Pesonen, P. 63
Peter the Great (Russia) 3
Piirainen, T. 65
Plamenatz, J. 12
pluralism 14, 22
Poland 9, 12, 30-1, 90
Polanyi, K. 81
populism 50-3
Portugal 48
post-communism 88
post-communist states 8-9, 17-27, 31-4
post-Finlandization 69
post-socialism 80-1, 90-1
poverty 28, 32-4
power: political 50, 88; Western 9, 13
Prague (Czech Republic) 3
pre-modernity 46
privatization 22, 26, 30-3, 82-3
productivity growth 28-9
protectionism 14
public sector 50, 67-8
Putin, V. 16-17
Putnam, R.D.: *et al.* 15
Pye, L. 15

Quijano, A. 10

racial equality 25
racism 12
radicalization 45, 54-5
Raik, K. 71
El Ramly, R. 72
rational actors 14
Renaissance 9
research-based education: new institutionalization (Finland) 67-9
rights: human 3, 22, 66, 73
Romania 12, 26, 33, 47-9, 81, 91
Rome (Italy) 1, 84
Rothschild, J.: and Wingfield, N.M. 3, 79
Rotkirch, A. 69
Rumsfeld, D. 47
Russia 3-5, 9, 15-20, 61-71, 88, 91; Aleksanteri Institute 65-7, 71; Moscow

5; Peter the Great 3; Putin 16-17; St Petersburg 88; Tsar Alexander I 61; Tsarist 2; Vladivostok 5
Russian studies 59-78
Russo-Japanese War (1905) 3

Saarikoski, V. 72
Sachs, J. 16
St Petersburg (Russia) 88
Sákharov, A. 88
Sanader, I. 26
Sarkozy, N. 47
Scandinavia 13
Schröder, H.-H. 80
science: politics of 59-67; social 14, 59, 65-6, 85-6
Segert, D. 1-4, 79-94; Dale, G. and Miklóssy, K. 1-6
Serbia 8, 12, 32, 91
serfdom 7, 10, 14
Seth, S. 10
seventeenth century 3
Shils, E. 12
sixteenth century 2, 21, 84
Slovakia 27, 30-1
Slovenia 8, 26-7, 30
Smith, A. 11
social Darwinism 55, 57n
social science 14, 59, 65-6, 85-6
socialism 57n, 81-2, 88-9; consumer 88; post- 80-1, 90-1; state 44, 52, 79-91
socialization 27
Soviet bloc 11, 14, 20, 79
Soviet Union (USSR) 9, 14, 62, 62-3, 88
Sovietological Studies 63
Sovietology 60-3, 73, 80
Spain 48
Spengler, O. 15
Stalinism 86
Stalinization 82
Stanley, M. 57n
state socialism 44, 52, 79-91
stereotyping 7, 13-16; cultural 11
stoicism 34
Strauss, F.-J. 62, 74n
Stykow, P. 80-1, 90
Süß, W. 88
Sugar, P. 12
Susiluoto, I. 63
Sutela, P. 63
Sweden 9; University of Södertörn 71
Szelenyi, I.: Townsley, E. and Eyal, G. 52

Teivainen, T. 72
Third World-ization 46
Tiltman, H. 11
Todorova, M. 90
Tolonen, J. 63

98

INDEX

Townsley, E.: Eyal, G. and Szelenyi, I. 52
Toynbee, A. 11, 15
transformative impacts of European
 Integration 22-6
transnational actors 89
Tsarist Empire 4, 10
Tsarist Russia 2
twentieth century 3, 81-3

Ukraine 56n, 71
ultra-nationalism 5, 17-19
unilateralism 23
United Kingdom (UK) 31, 61; Birmingham
 Centre of Russian and East European
 Studies 67; Cameron 47; London 3;
 University College London School of
 Slavonic and East European Studies (UCL
 SSEES) 67-8
United States of America (USA) 11, 31, 84
University College London (UCL) School of
 Slavonic and East European Studies
 (SSEES) 67-8
University of Helsinki (Finland) 61, 72, 75n
University of Södertörn (Sweden) 71
USSR (Union of Soviet Socialist Republics)
 9, 14, 62, 62-3, 88
utopia 87

Verdery, K. 81; and Burawoy, M. 81
Vienna (Austria) 2, 92n; Josefstadt 3
Vihavainen, T. 65, 69
Vladivostok (Russia) 5

Warsaw Pact (1955) 11
Weber, M. 11, 15
West 3-5, 7-11, 14-17, 44-6, 62-5, 82-3,
 88-9
Western capitalism 56n
Western powers 9, 13
Wingfield, N.M.: and Rothschild, J. 3, 79
Wittfogel, K. 11
Wolff, L. 7-9, 79, 90
working class 55, 57n
World War I (1914-18) 3
World War II (1939-45) 8, 13-14, 62,
 83-5

xenophobia 8, 13, 19, 29, 34

Yeltsin, B. 16
Yurchak, A. 88-9

Zetterberg, S. 71
Zielonka, J. 23
Zinoviev, A. 15